I believe that art is a universal form of communication that helps us focus on life and small details, and I am grateful to be able to share my art through these pages.

Numerimperdivel Unipessoal Lda©
Carlos Pais
2024

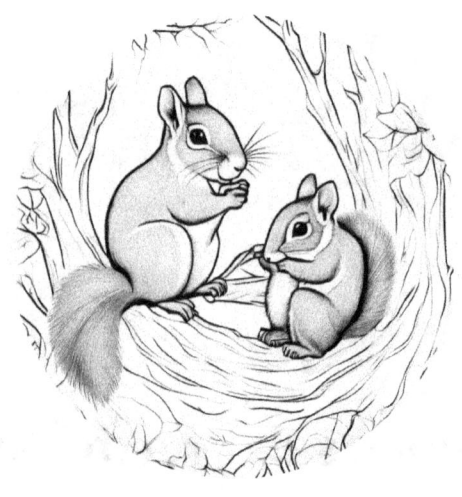 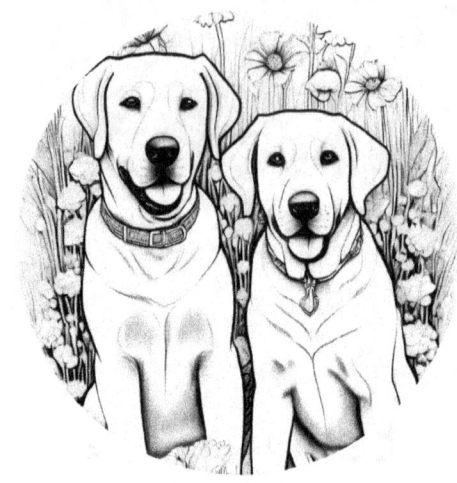

This Book Belongs To:

_____

All rights reserved
2024

No part of this publication may be reproduced, distributed, or trasmitted in any form or by any means, including photocopying, recording, or other electronic or mechanical methods, without the prior written permission of the publisher, except for brief quotations incorporated in critical reviews and other specific noncommercial uses. Any unanthorized replica of this work is prohibited.

Test Color Page

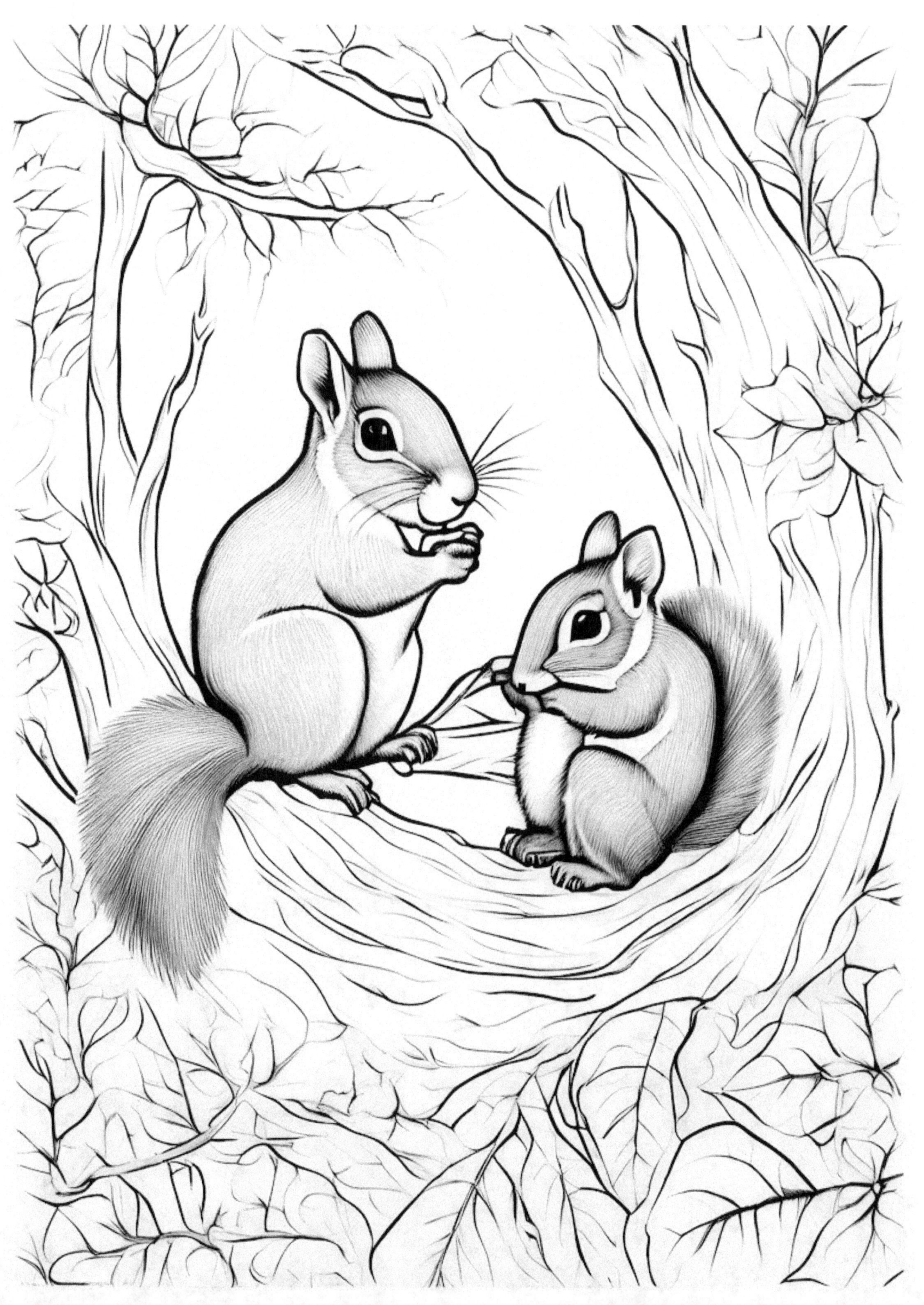

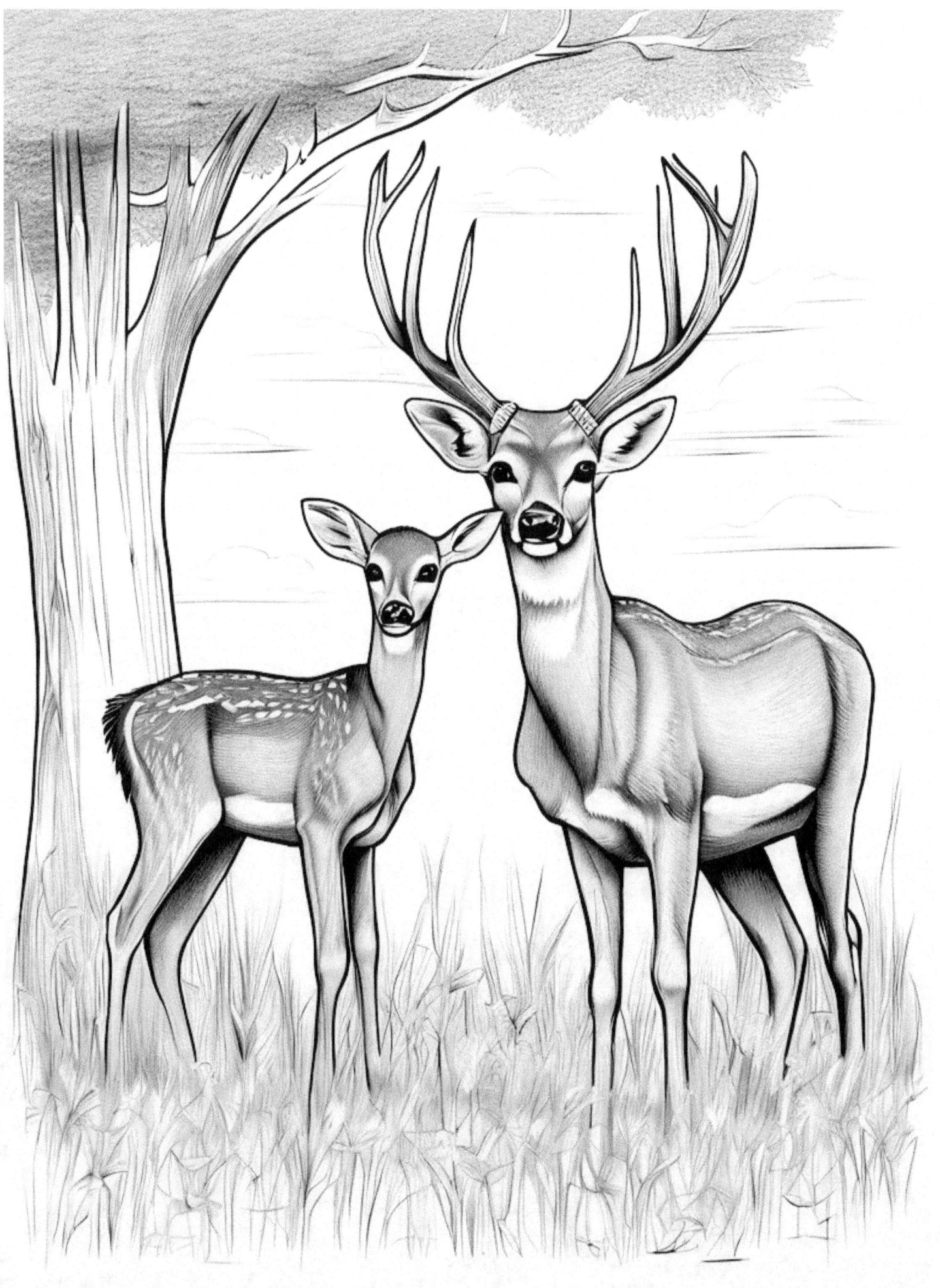

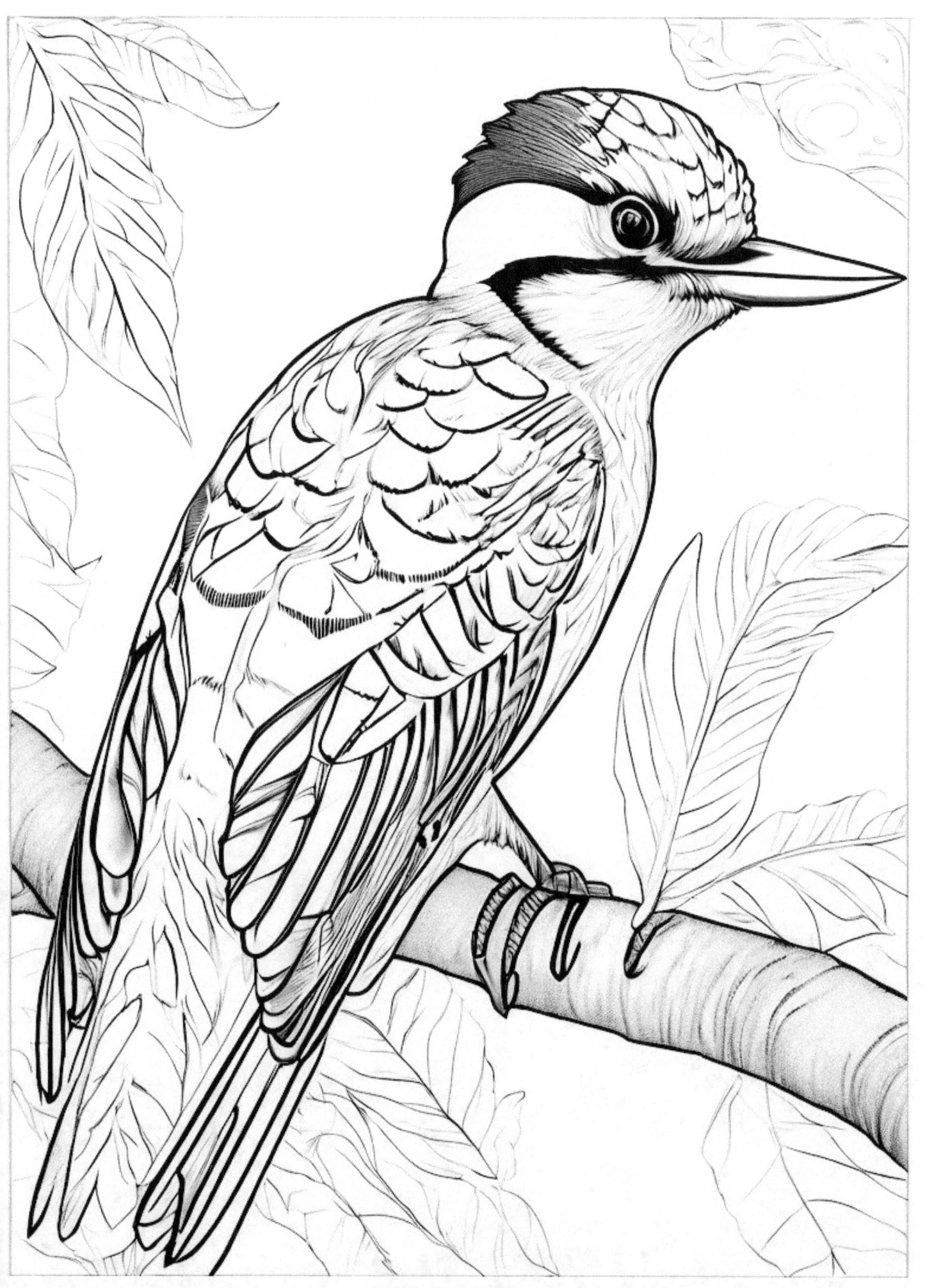

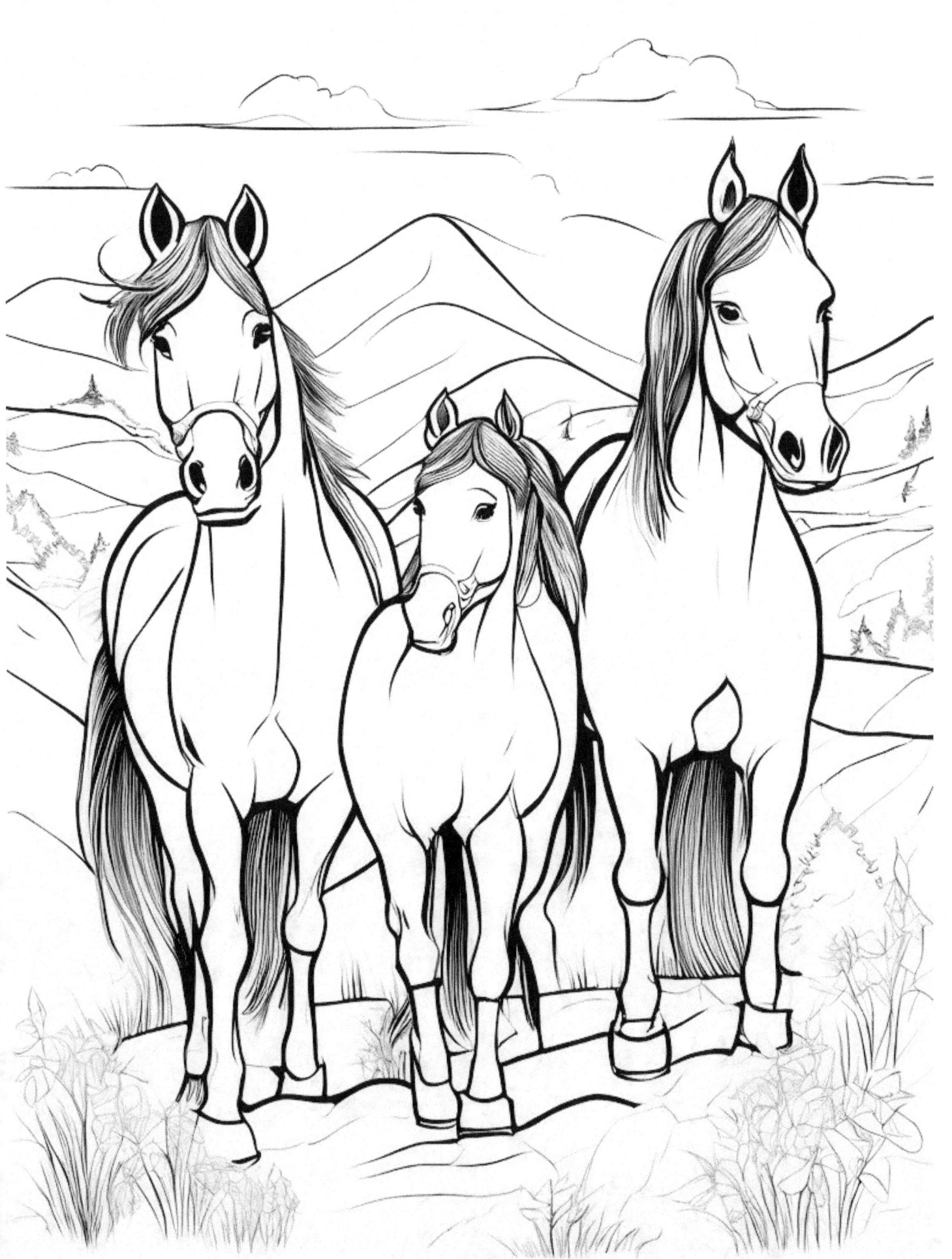

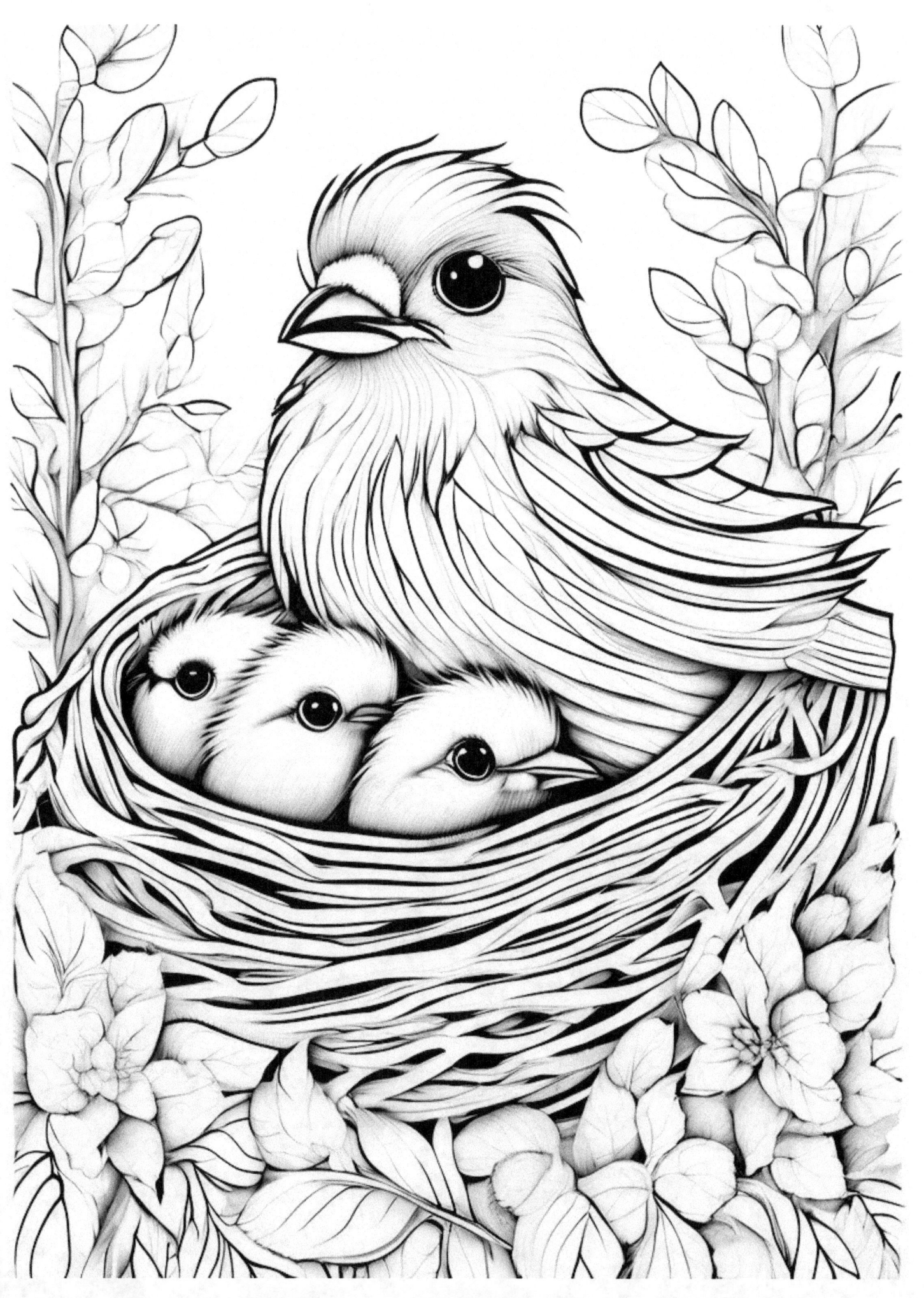

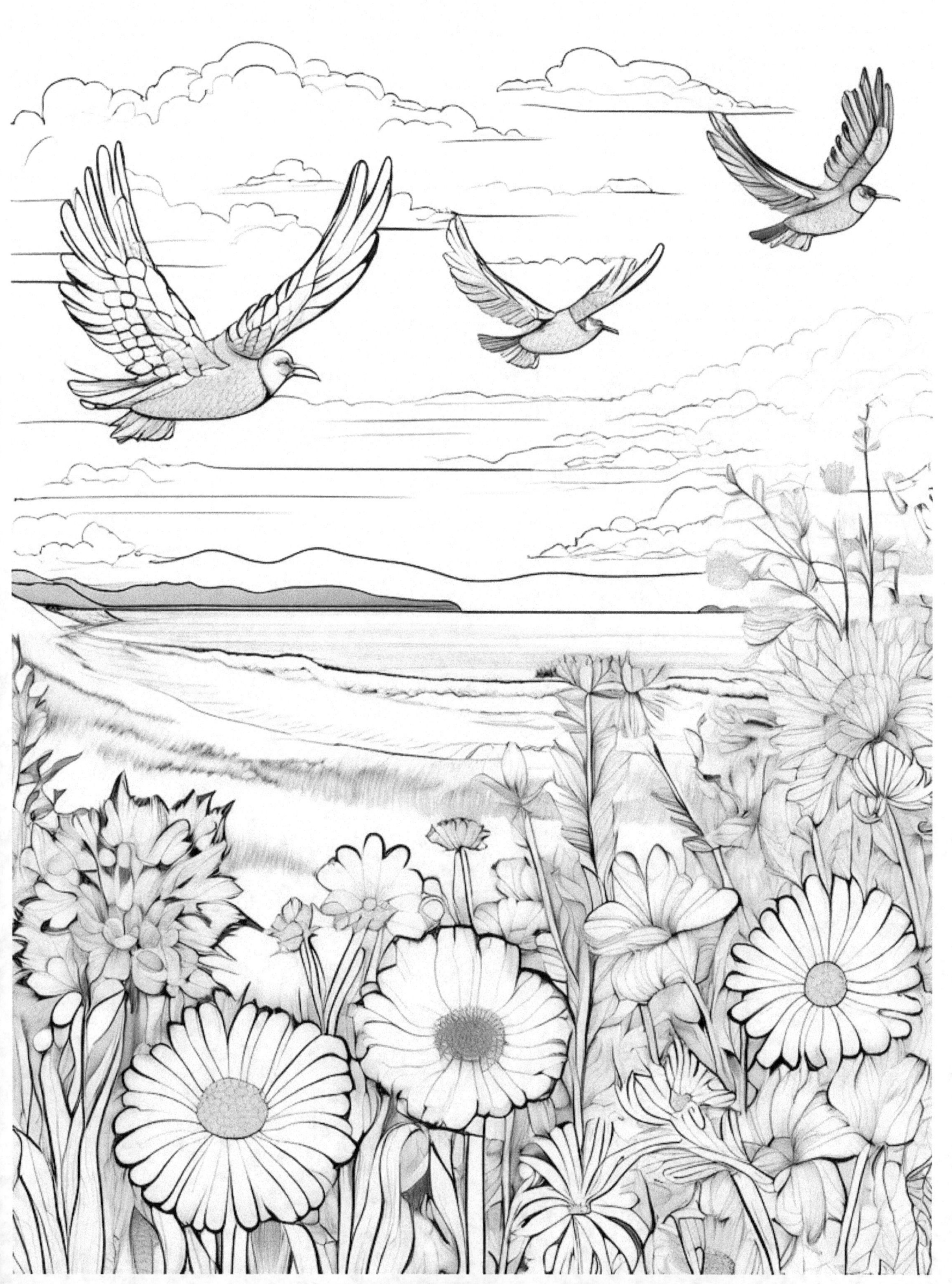

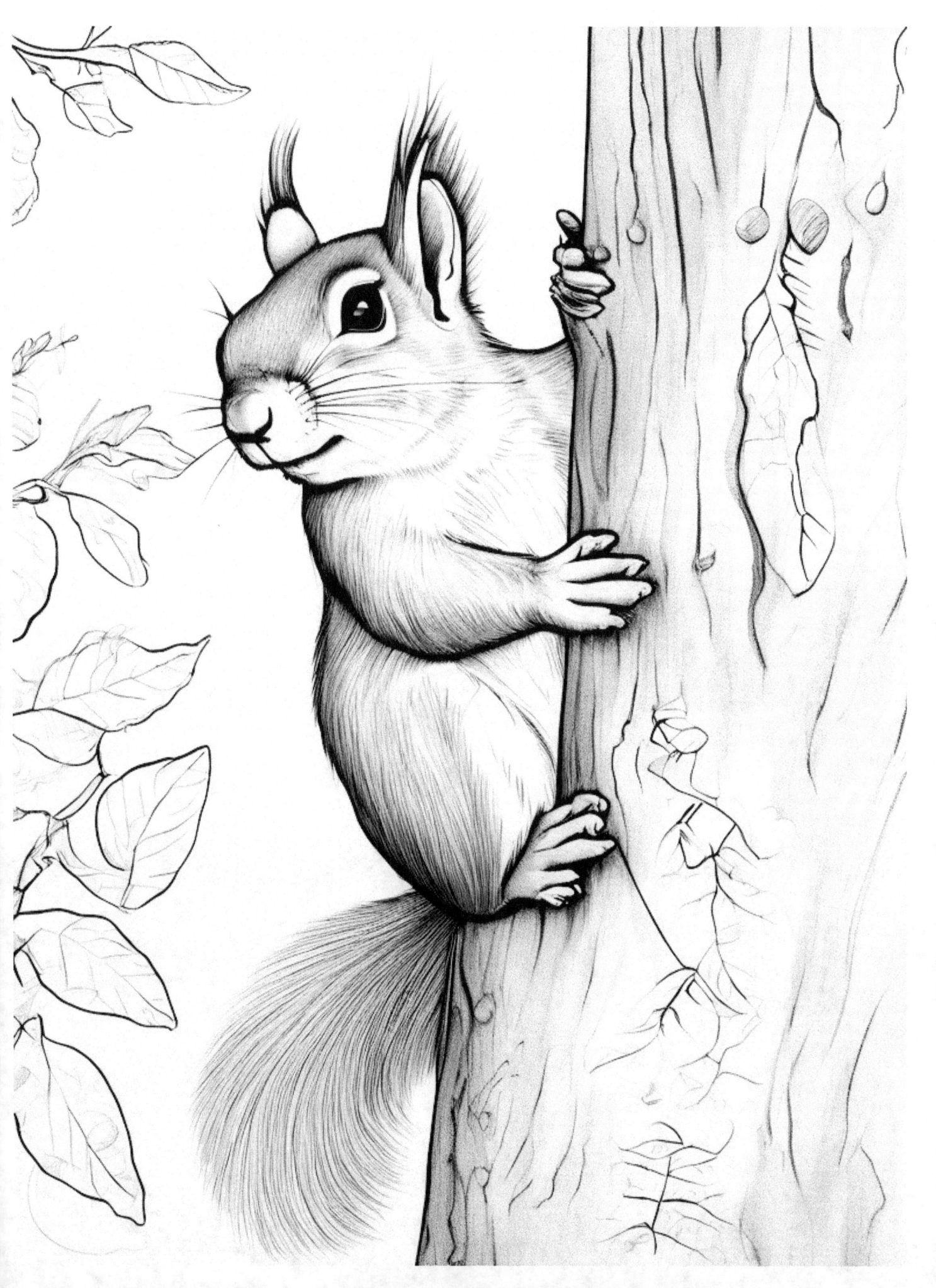

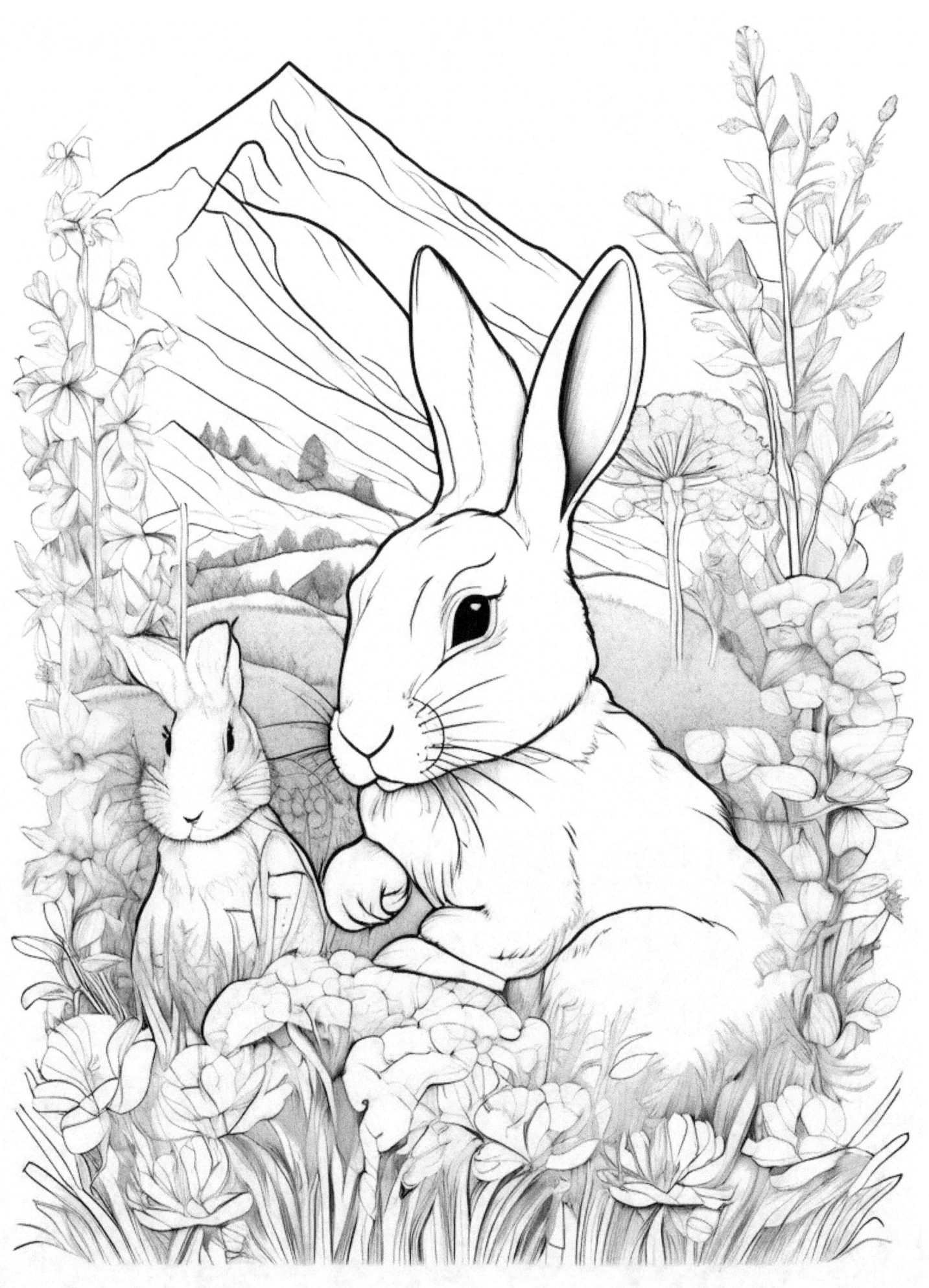

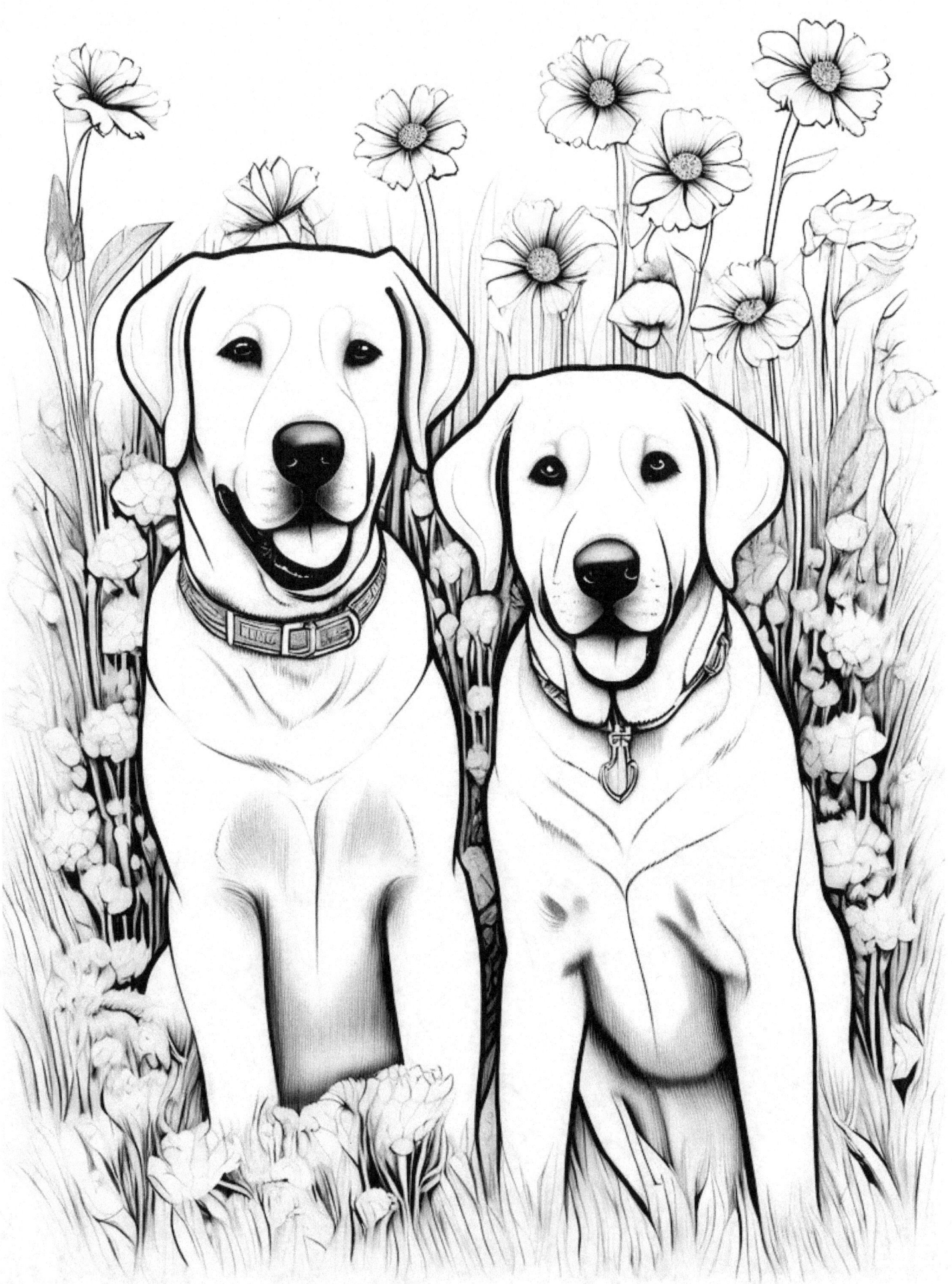

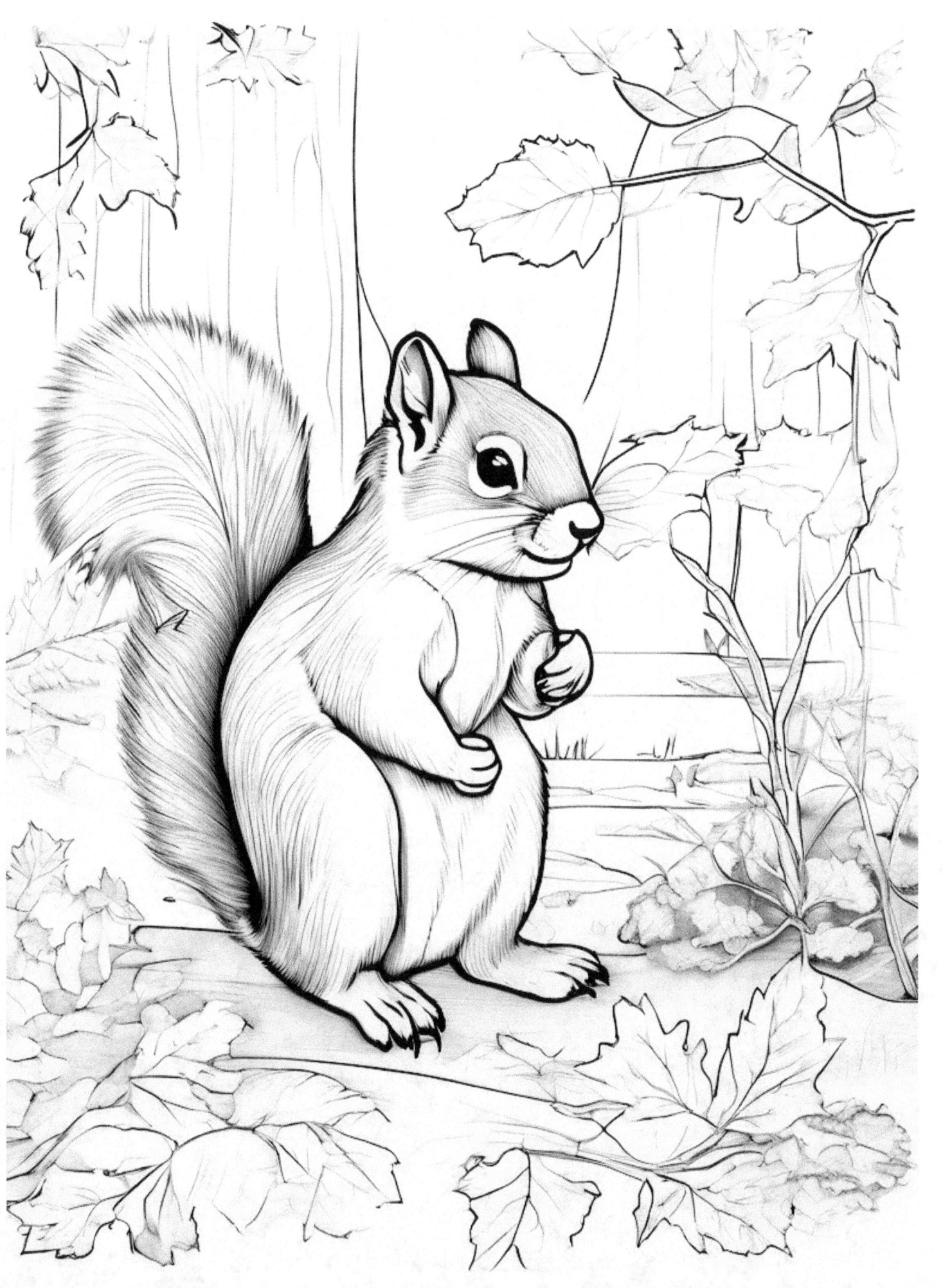

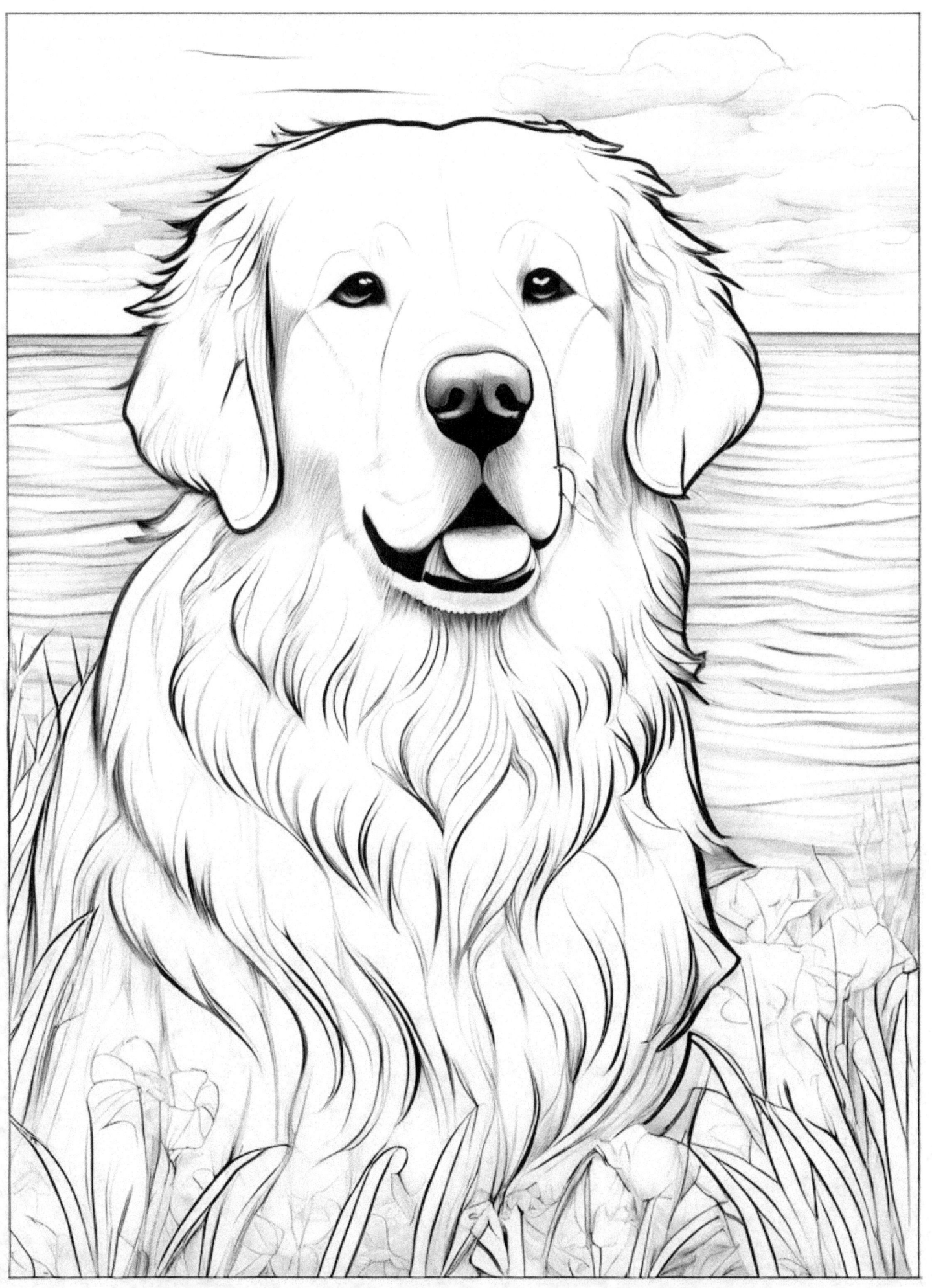

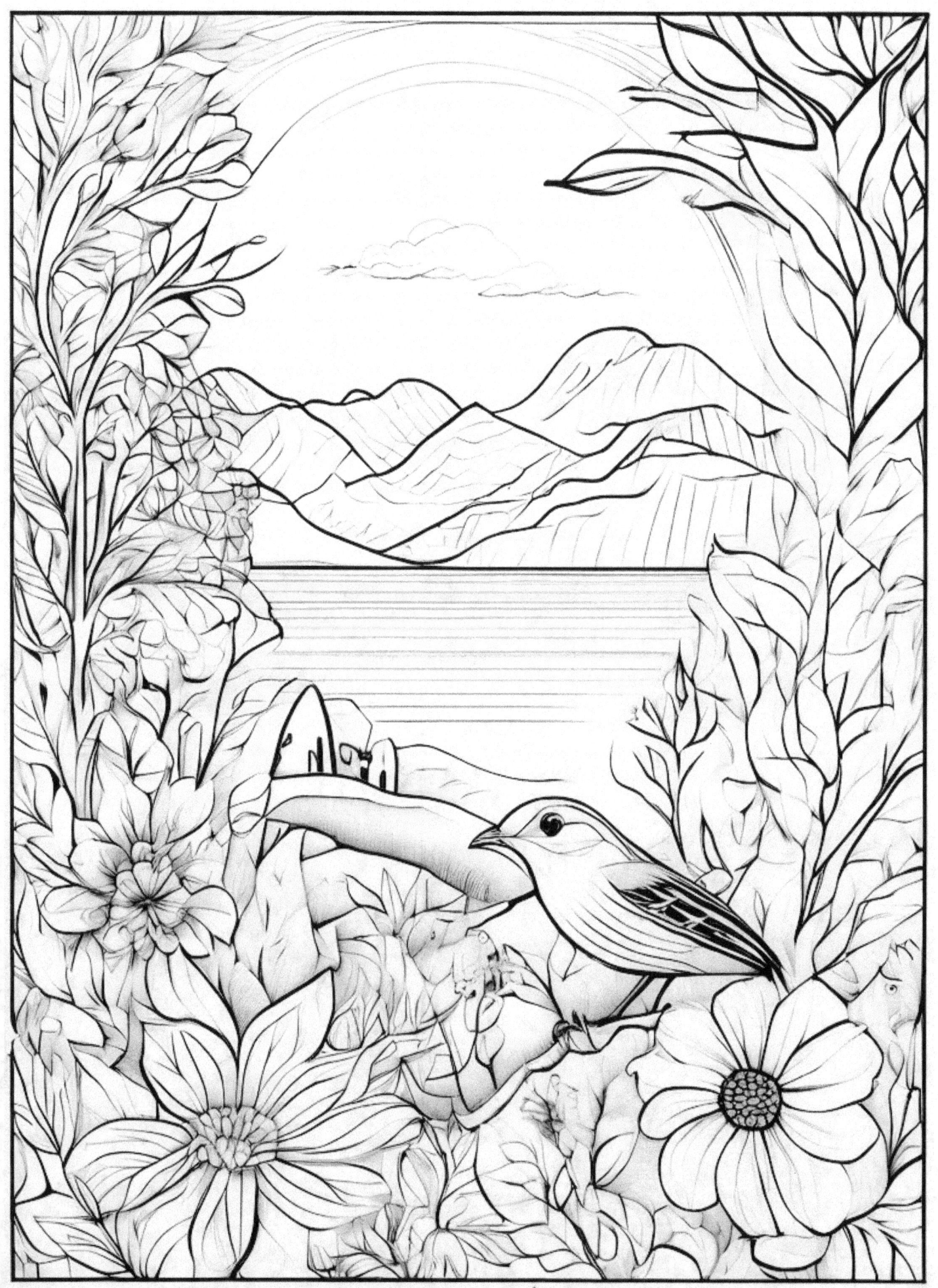

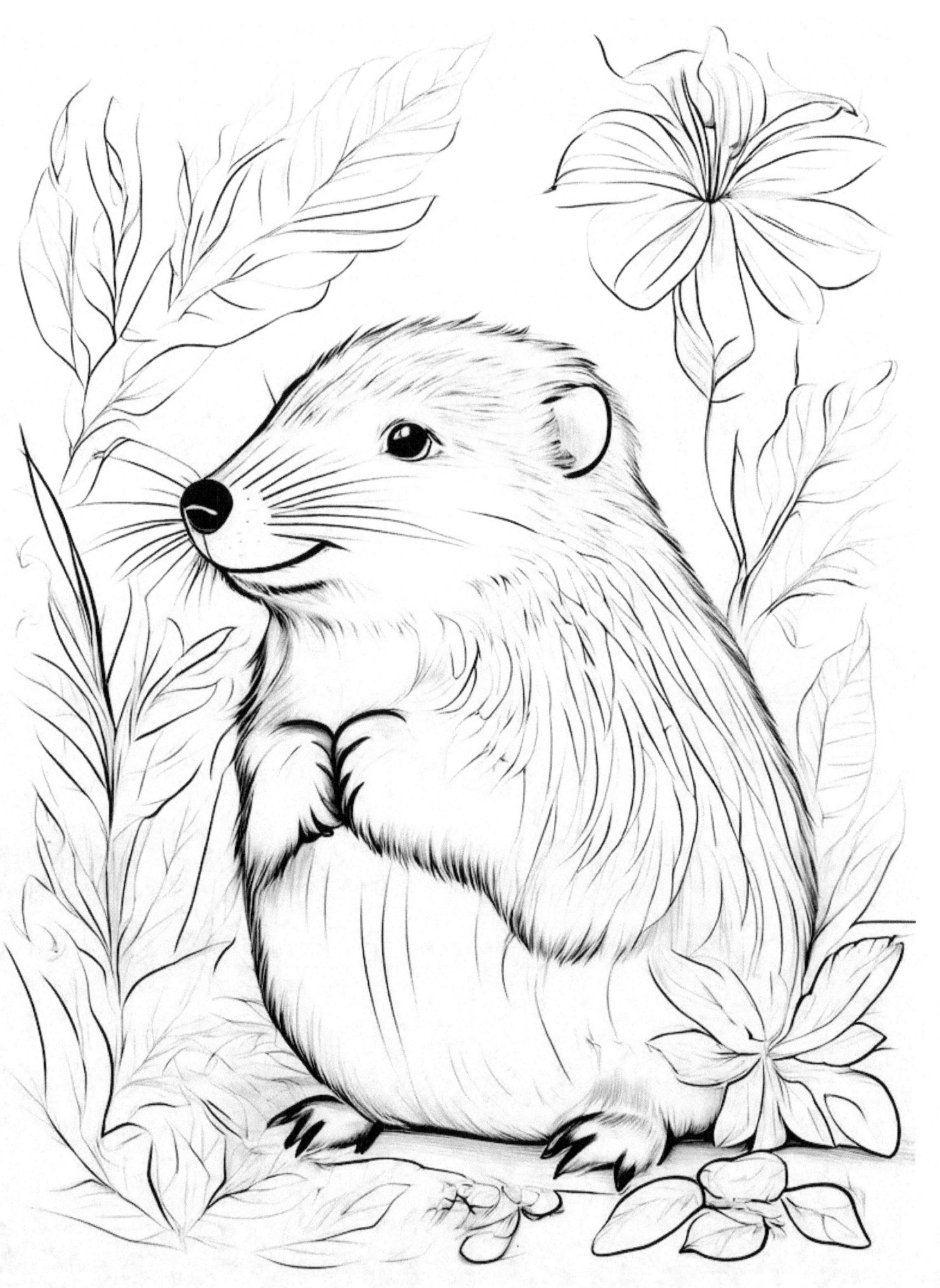

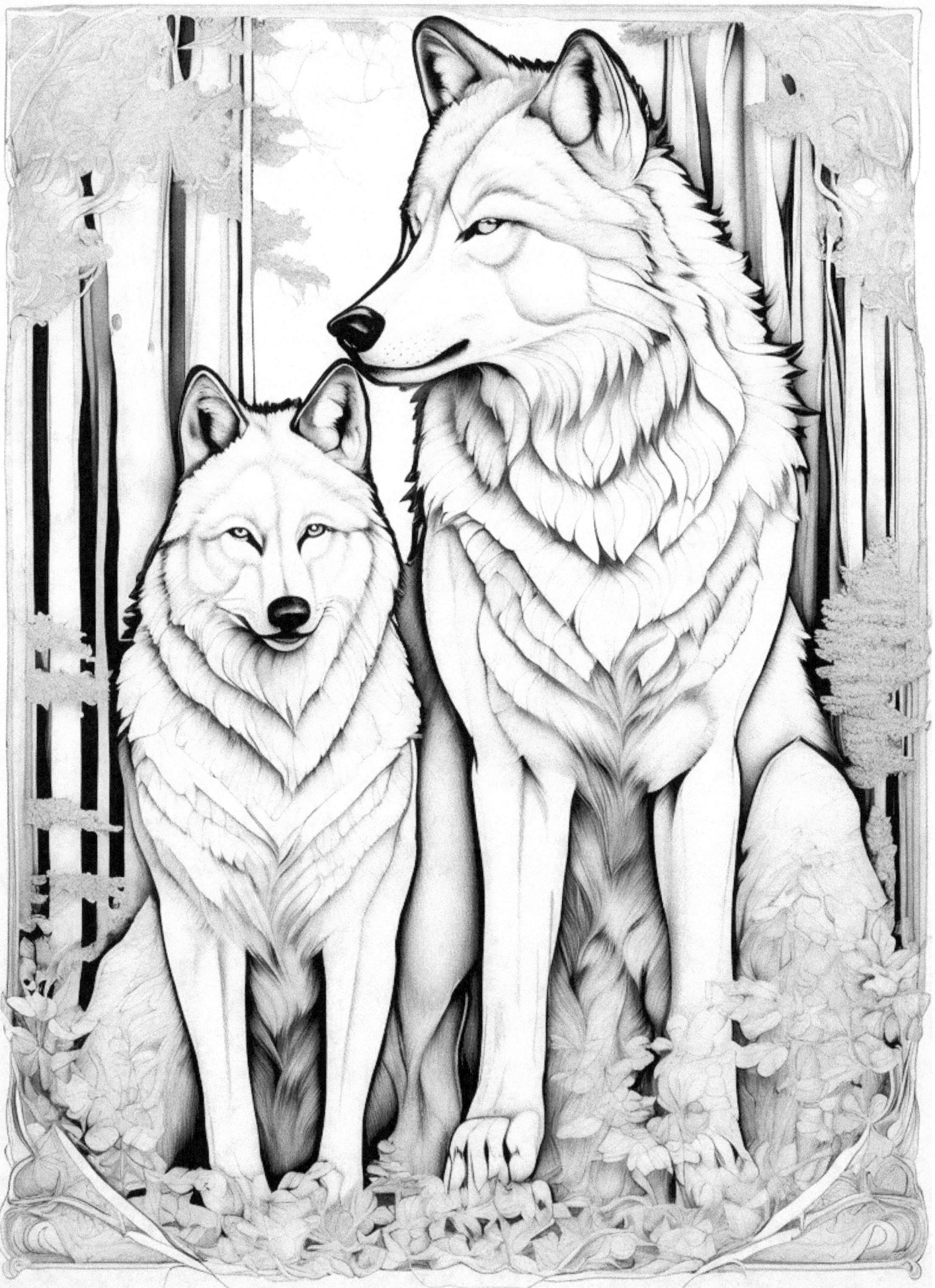

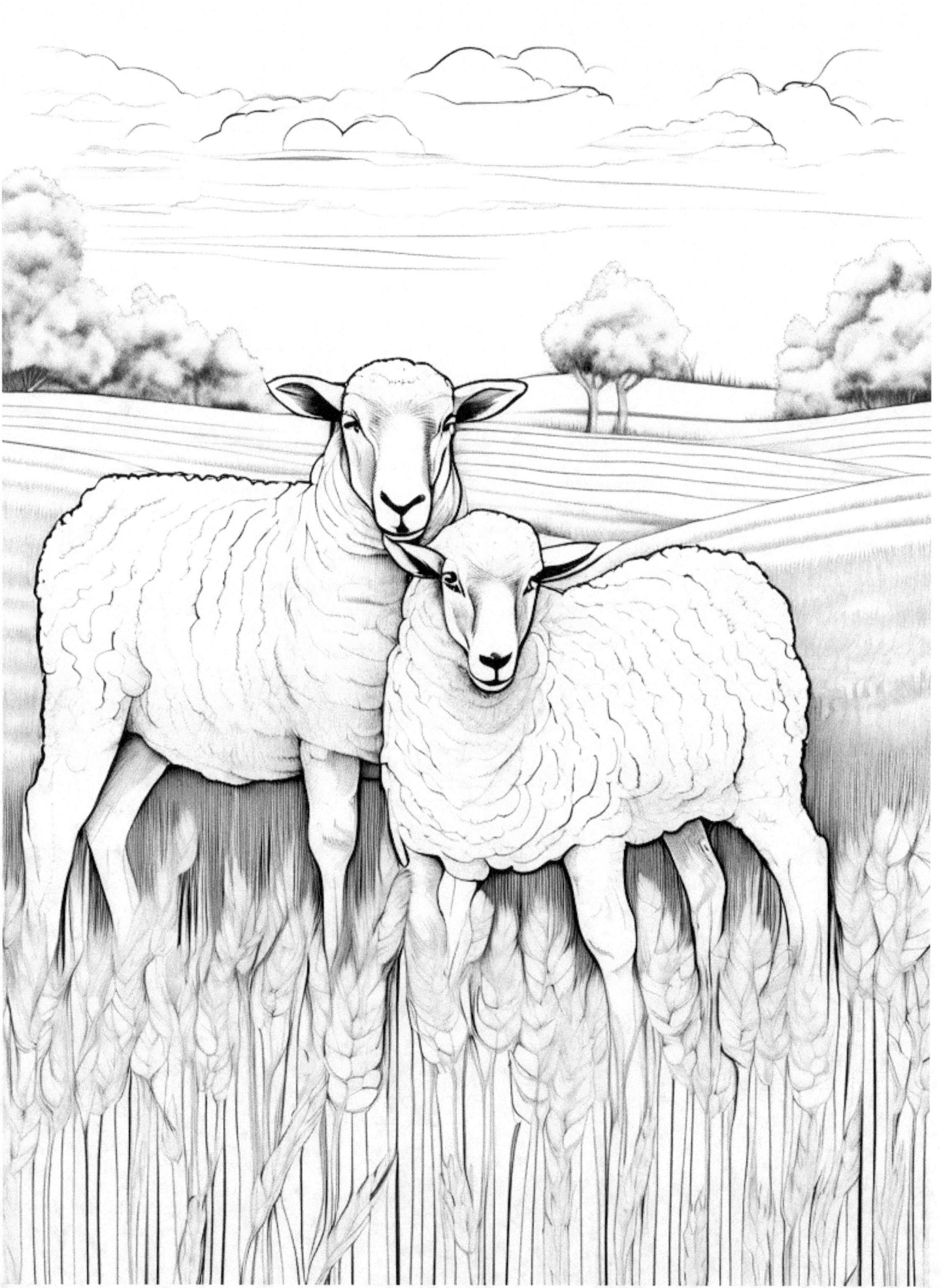

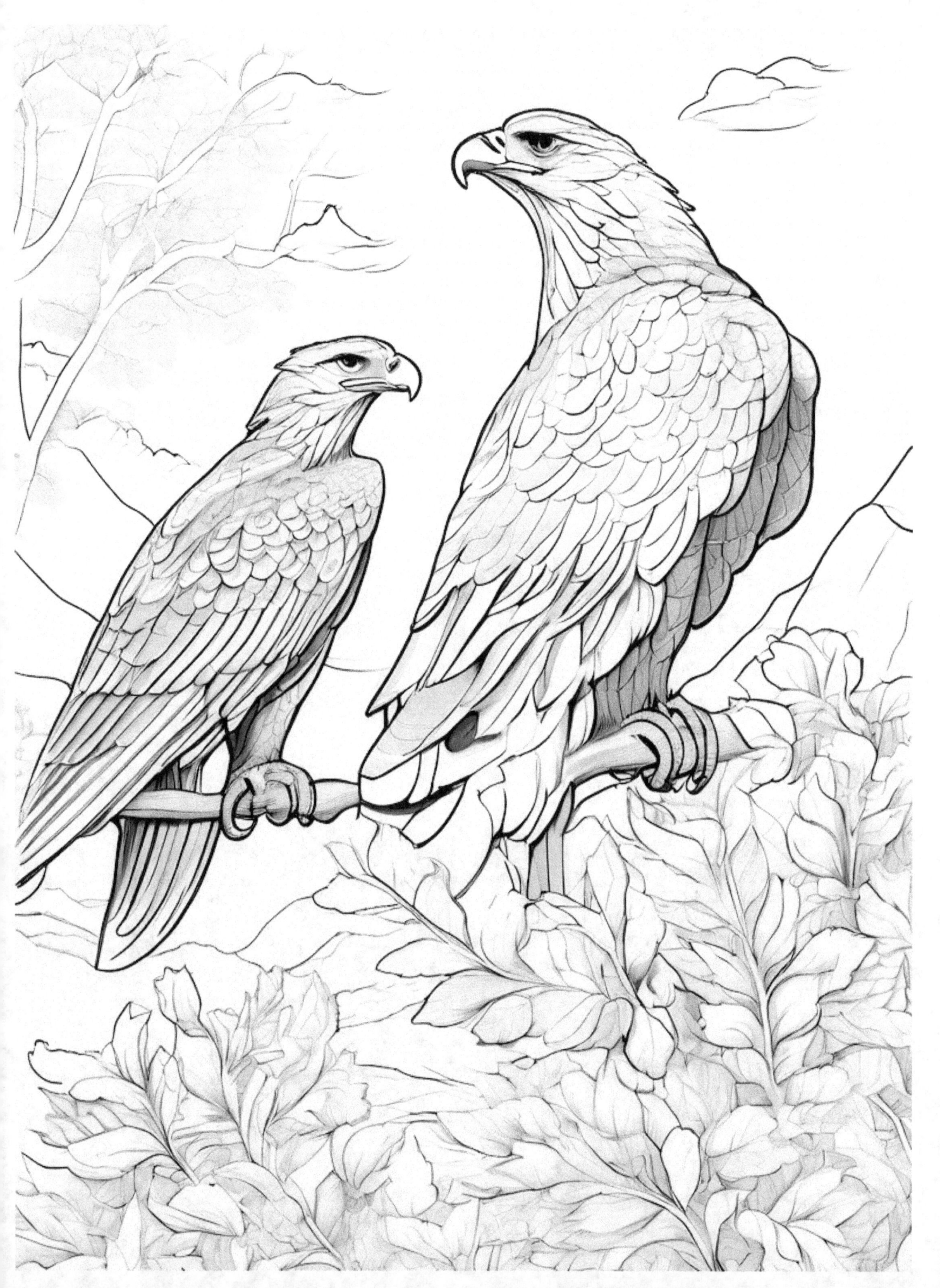

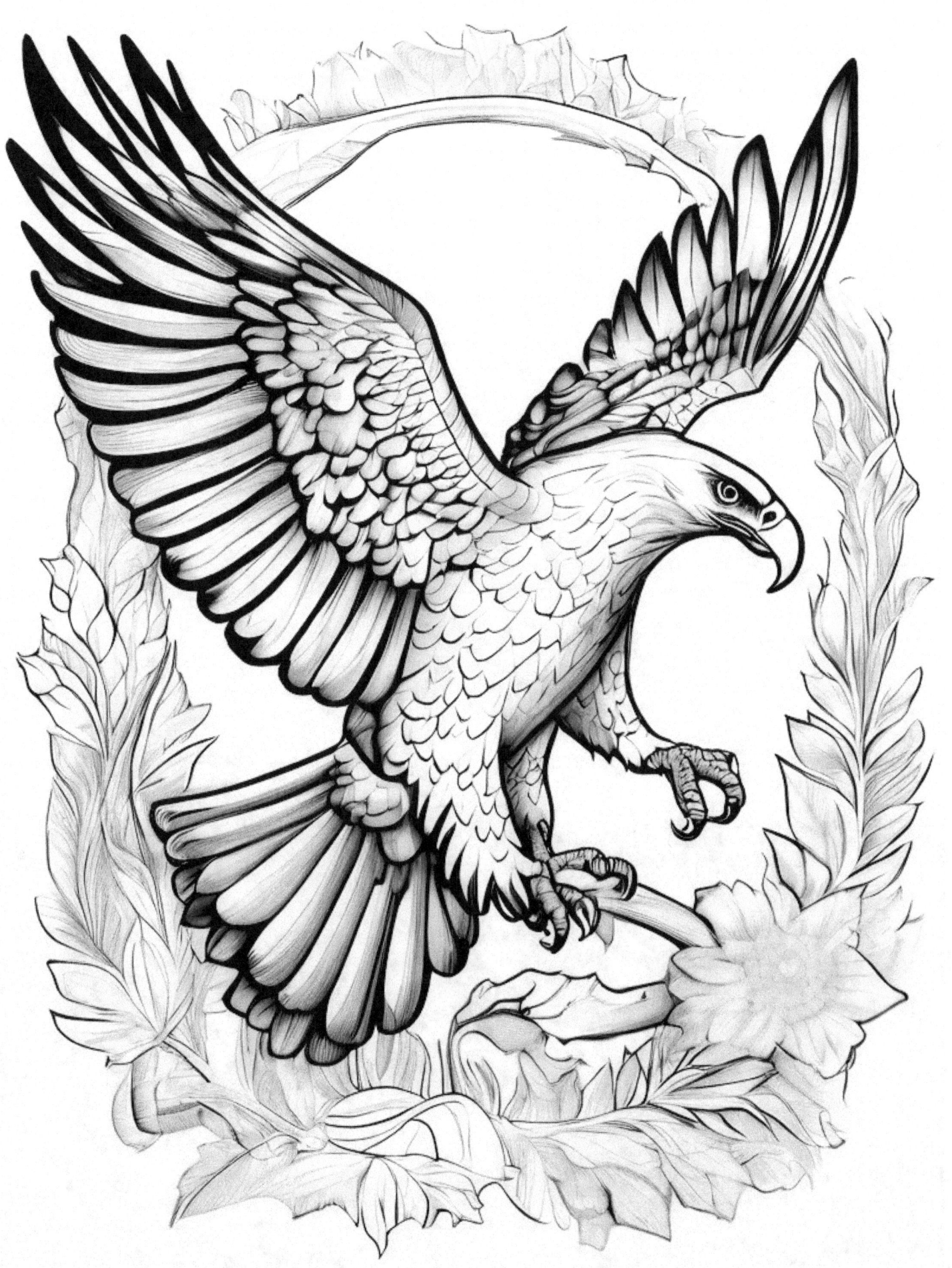

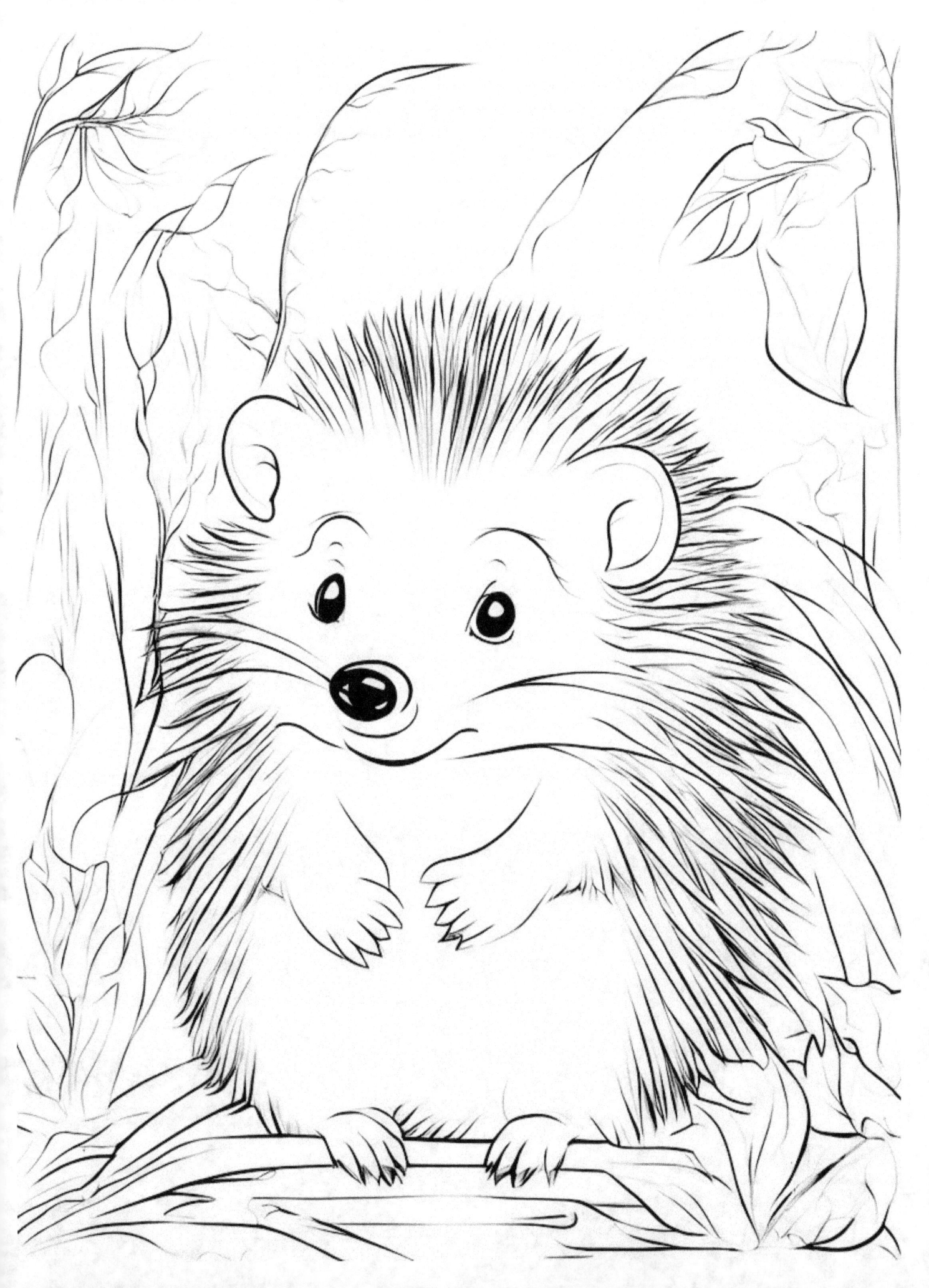

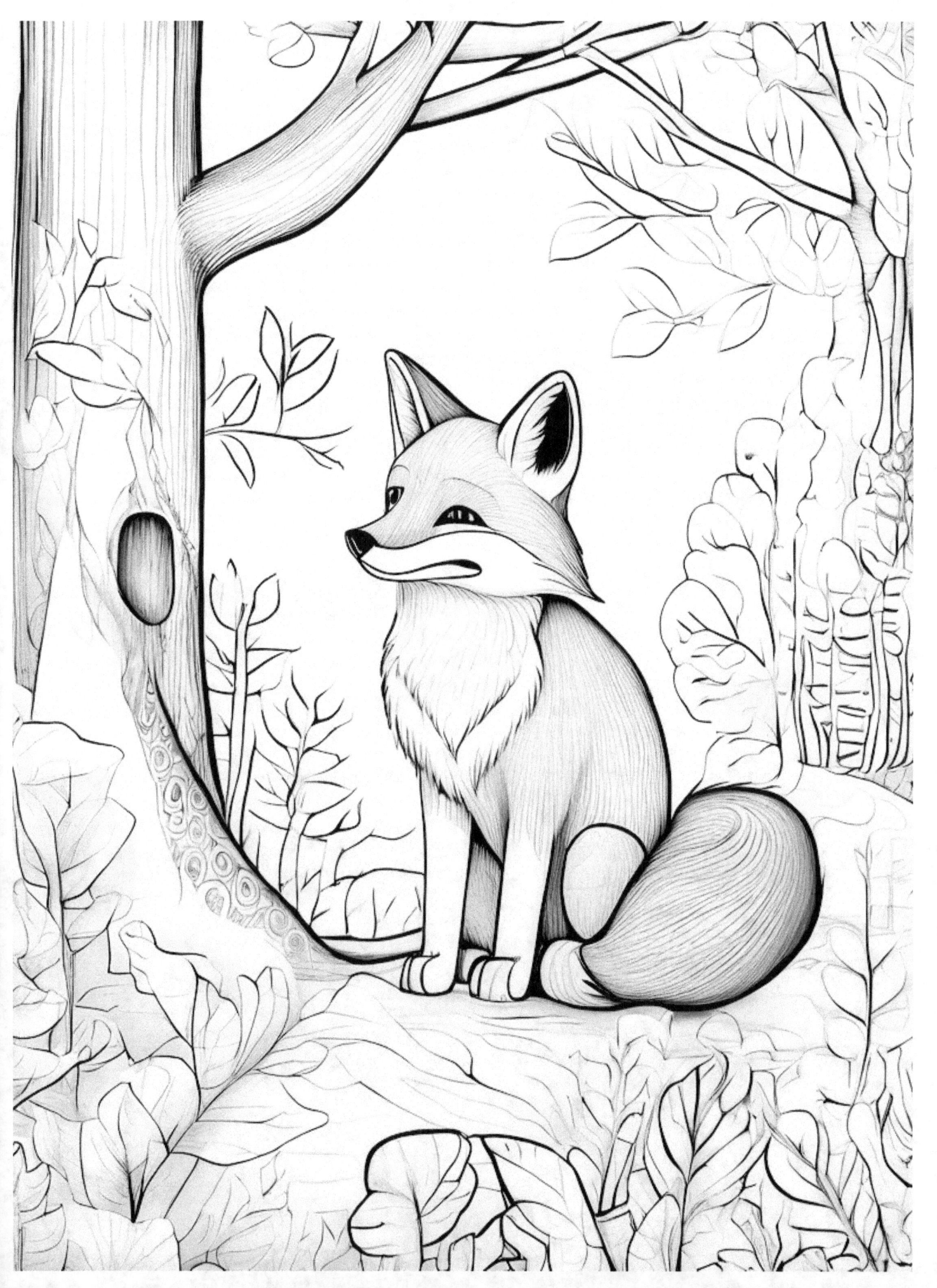

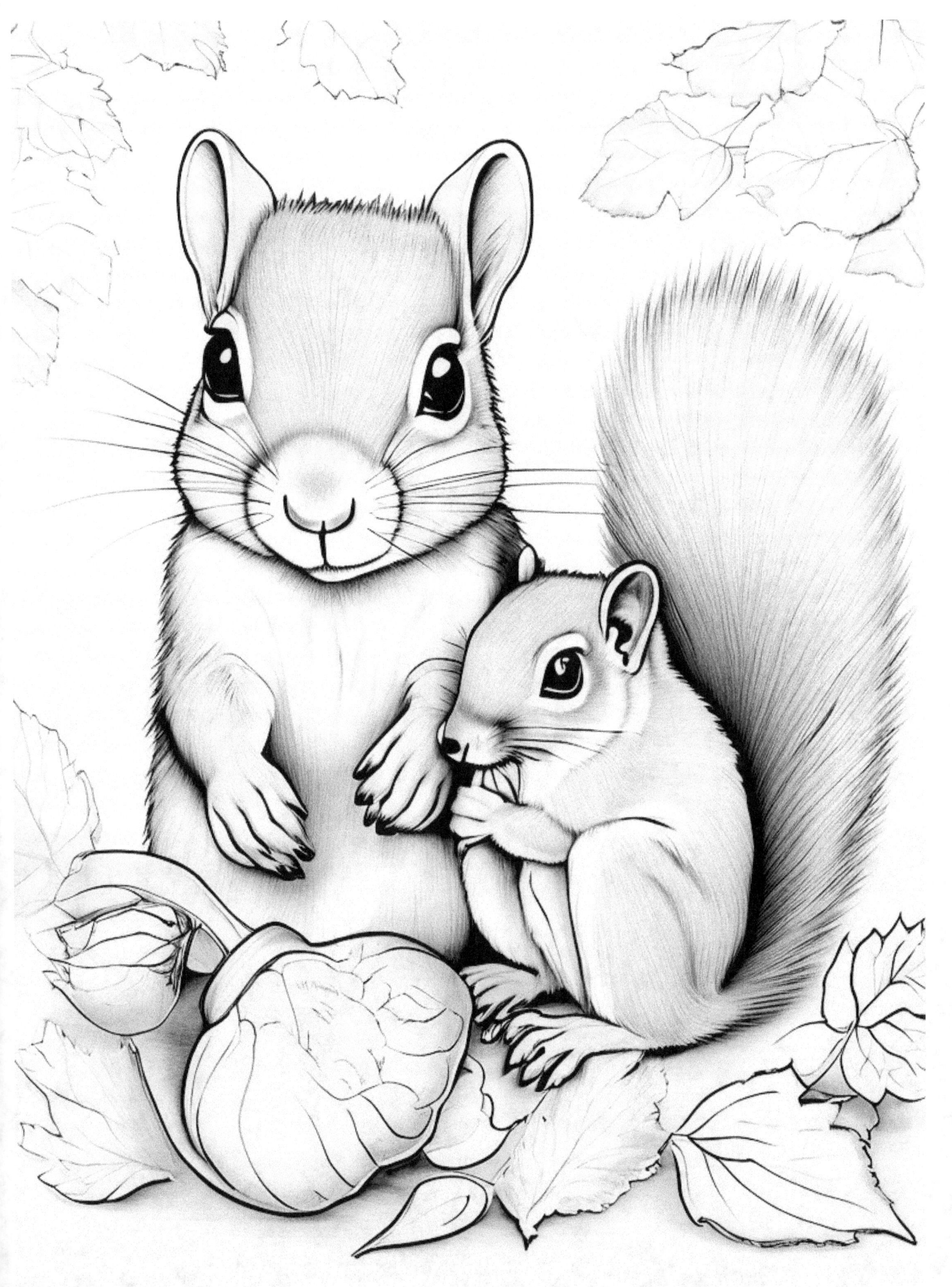

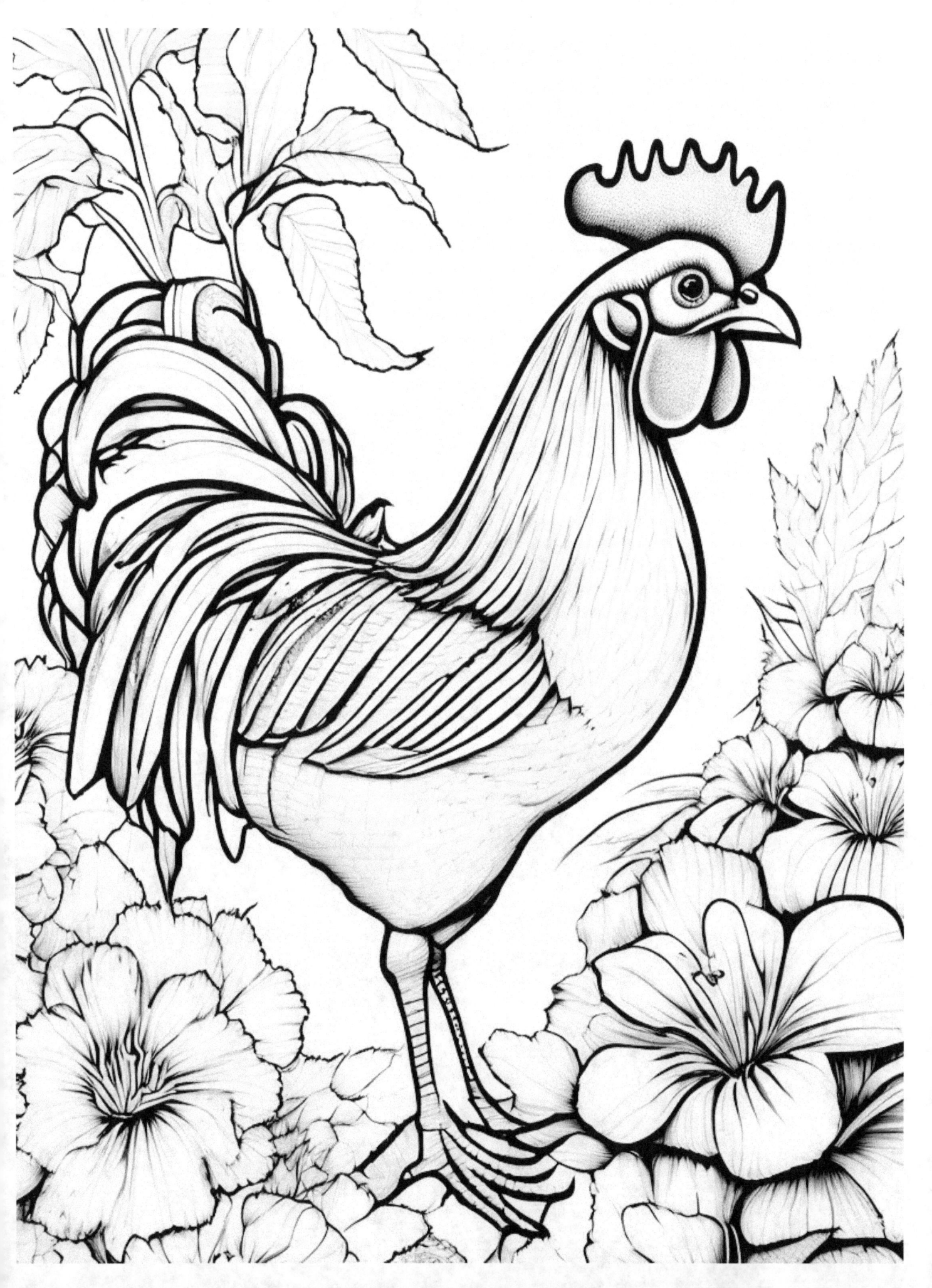

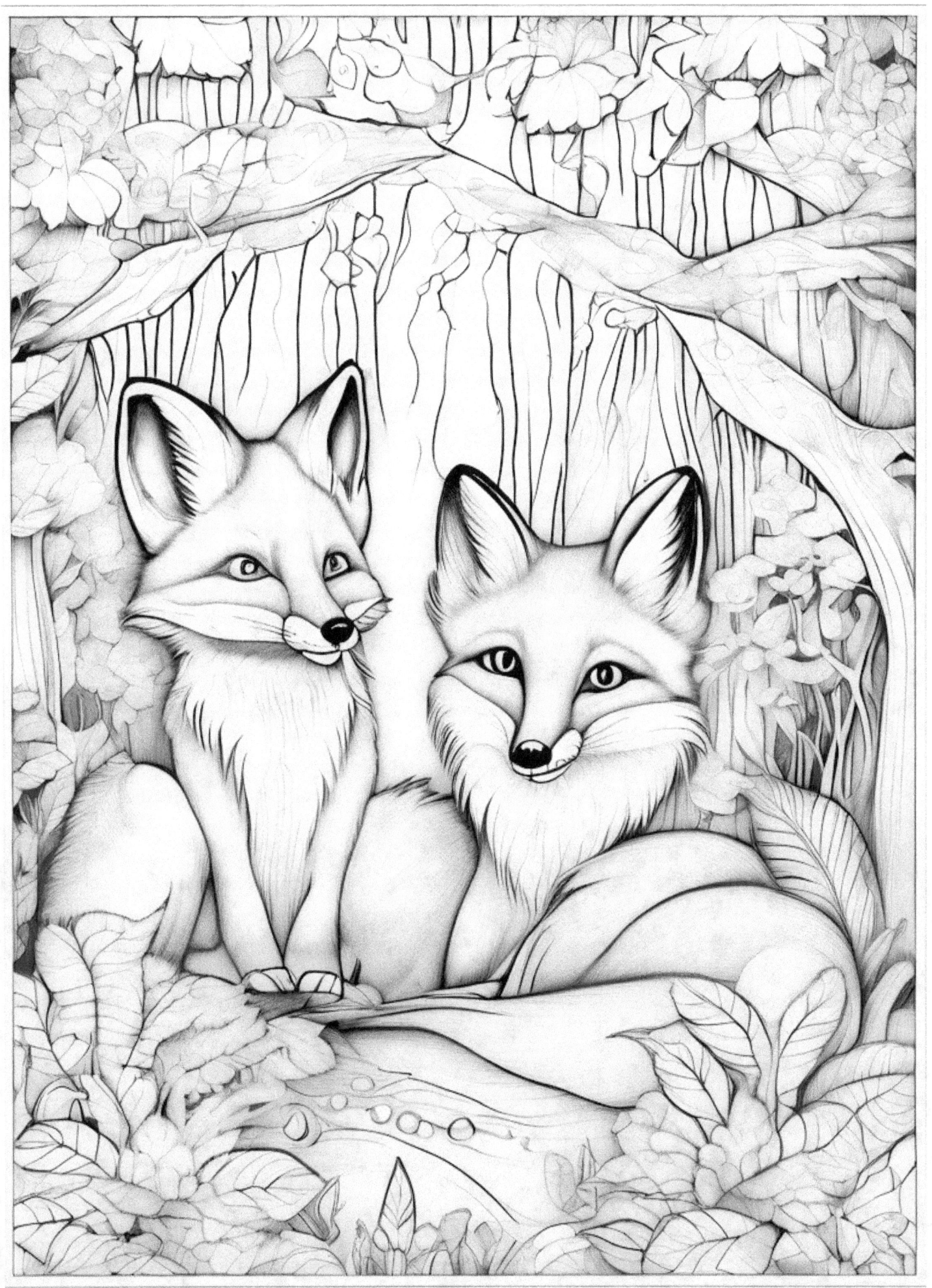

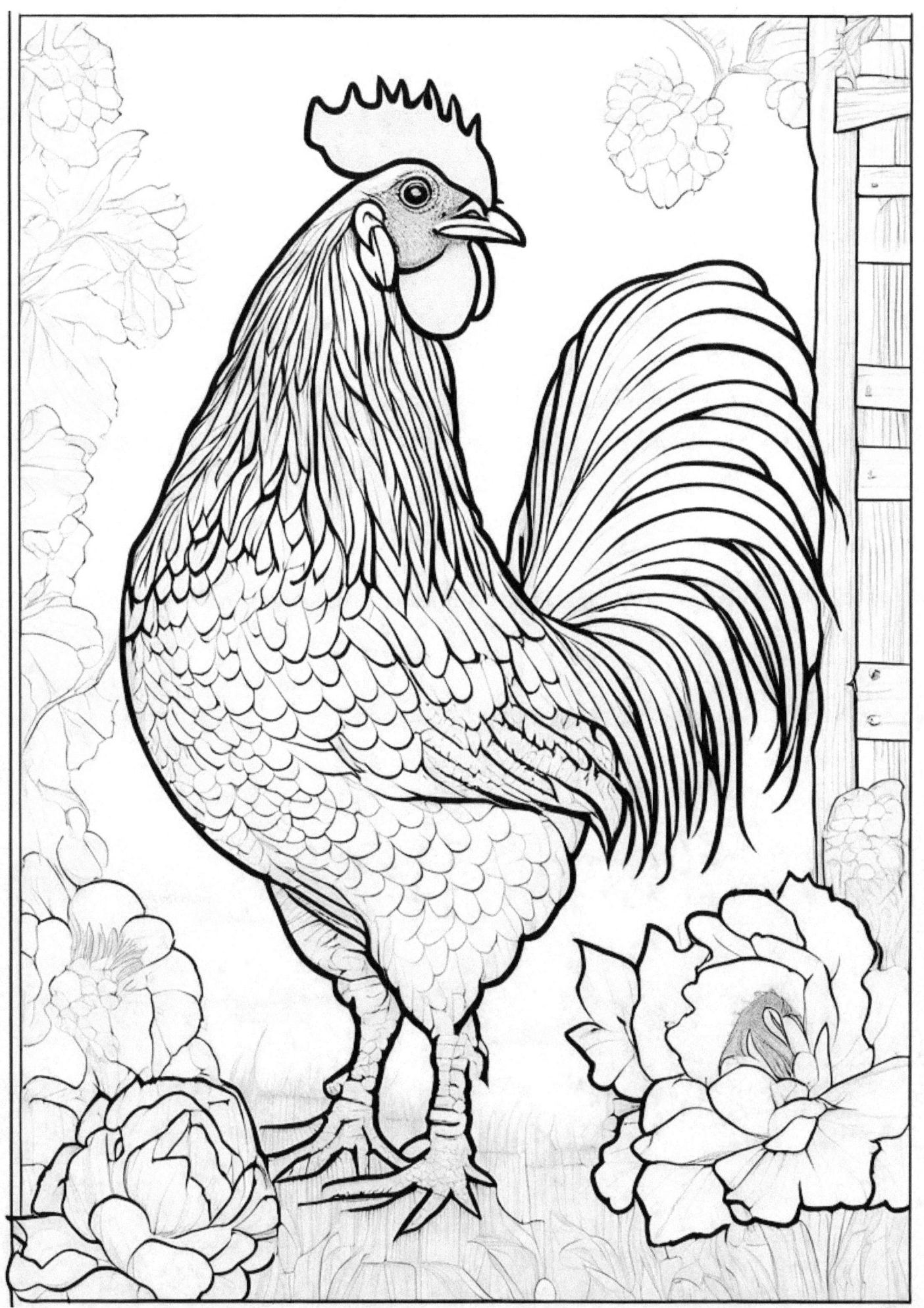

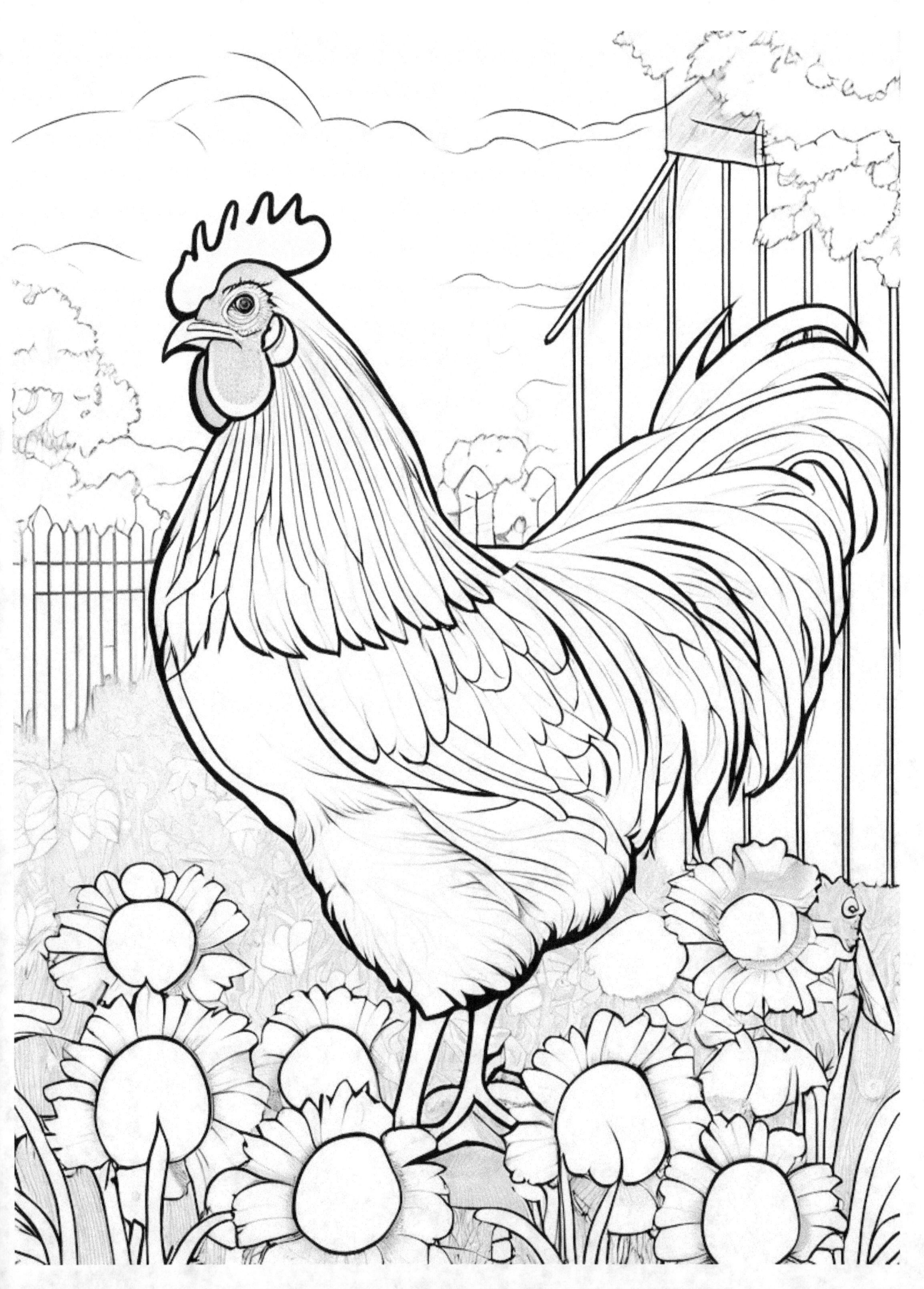

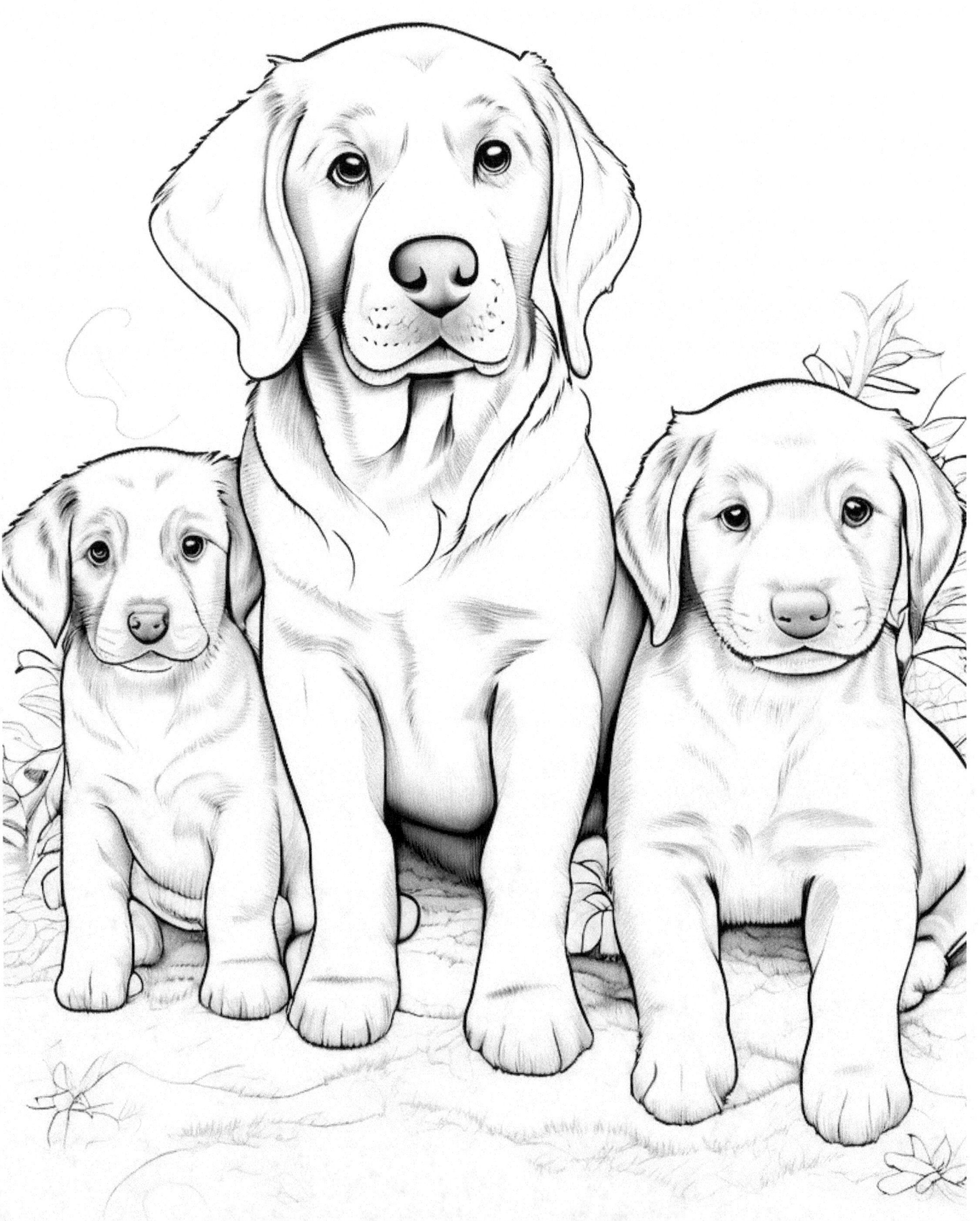

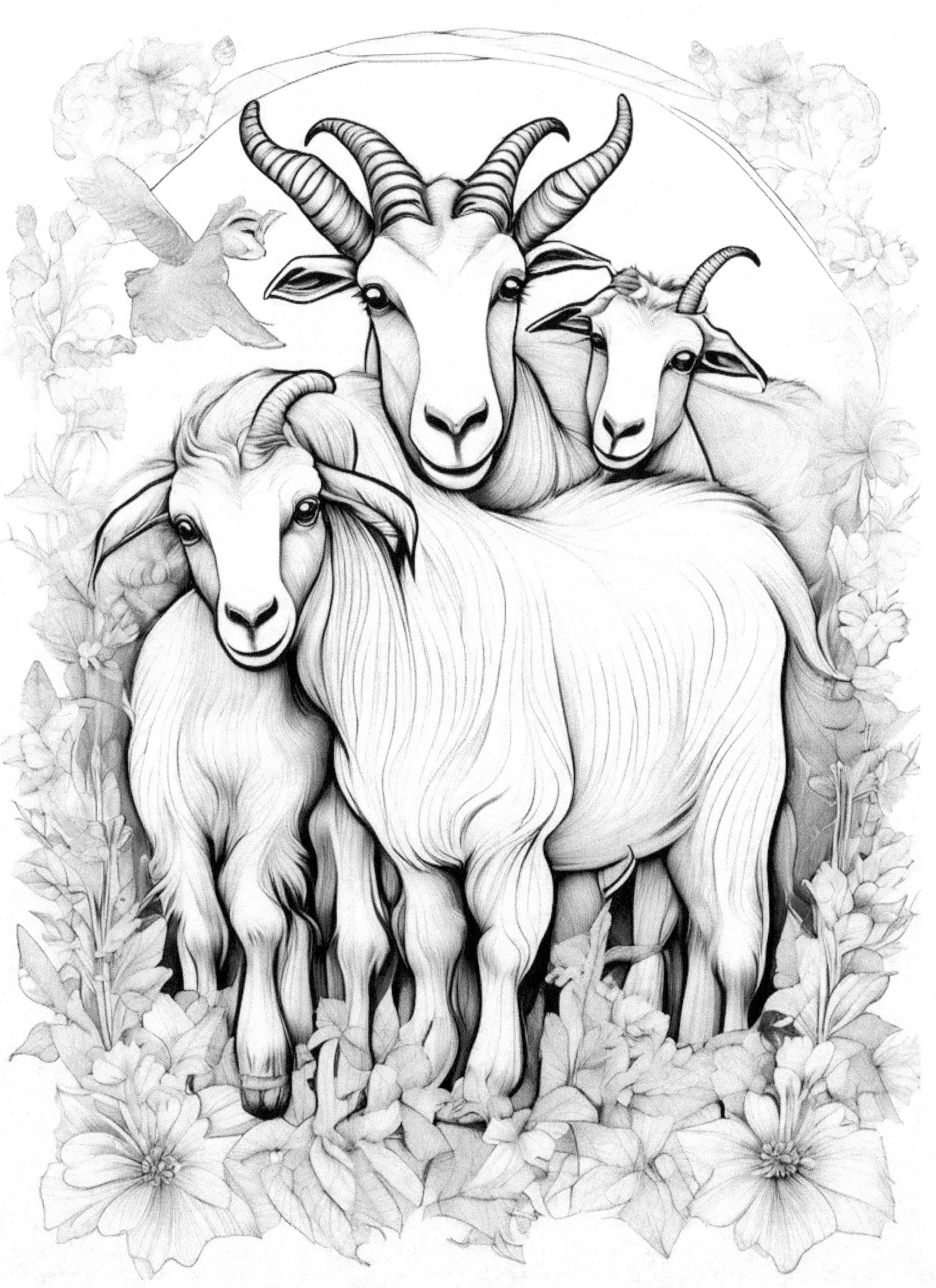

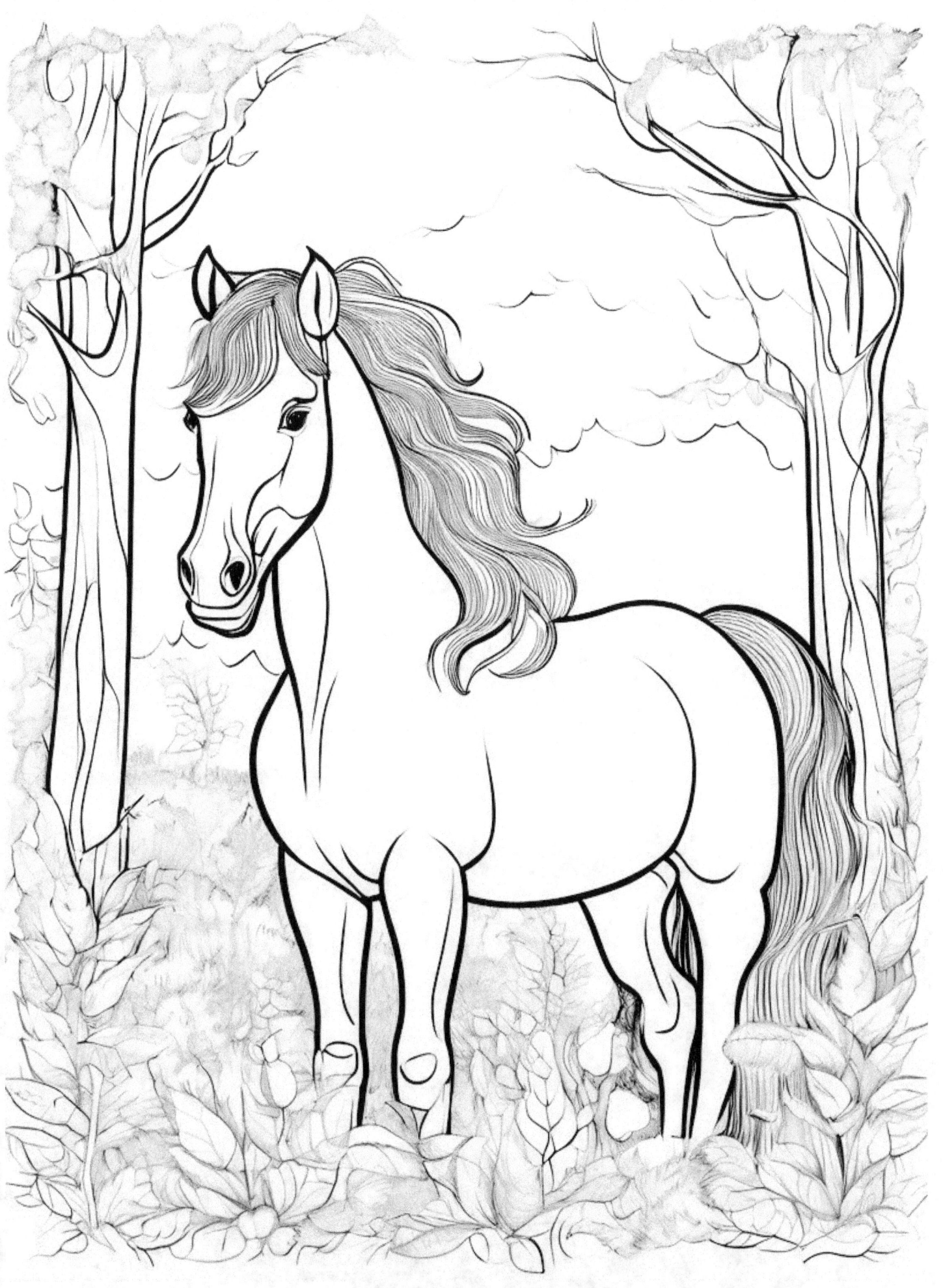

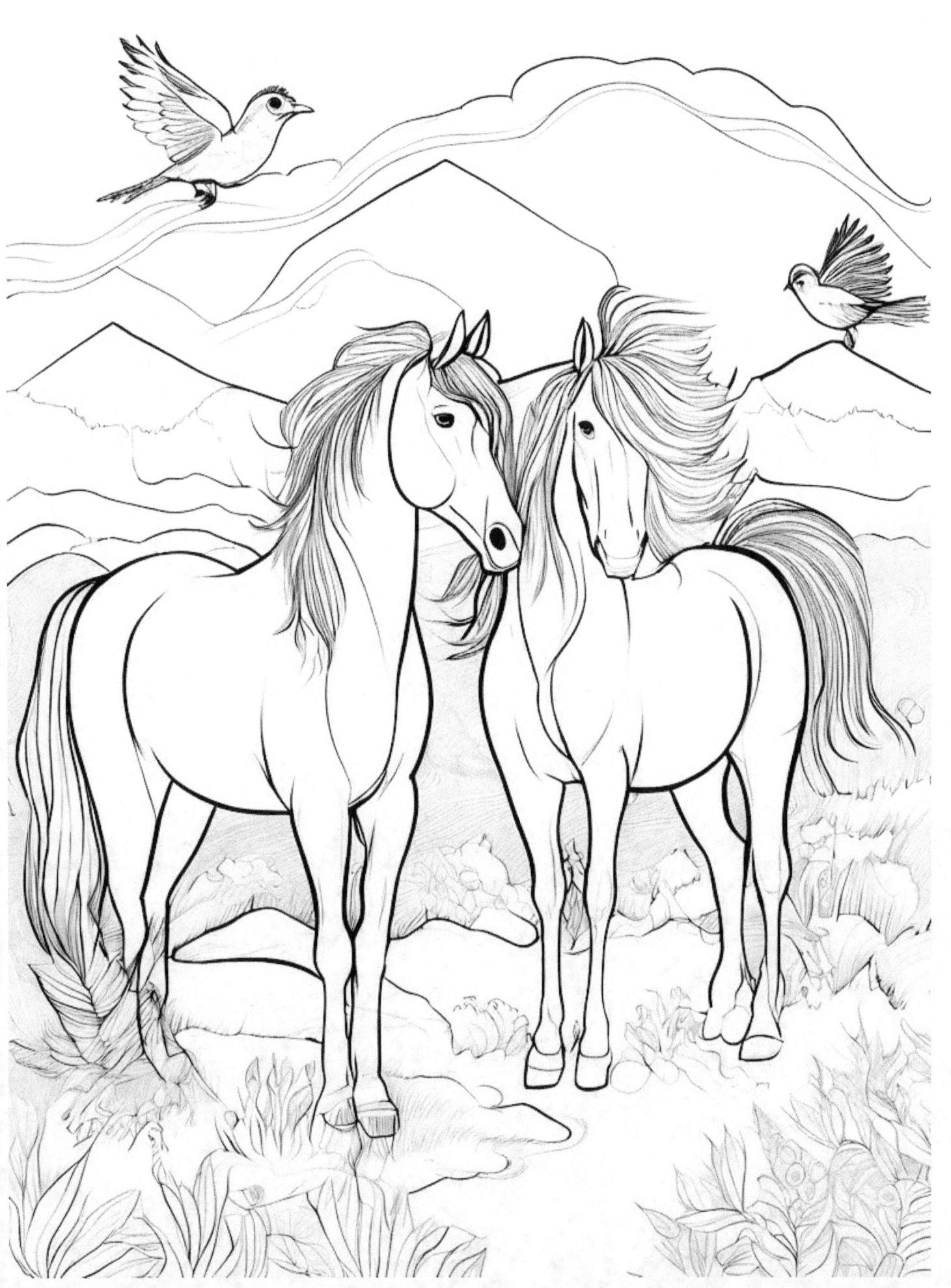

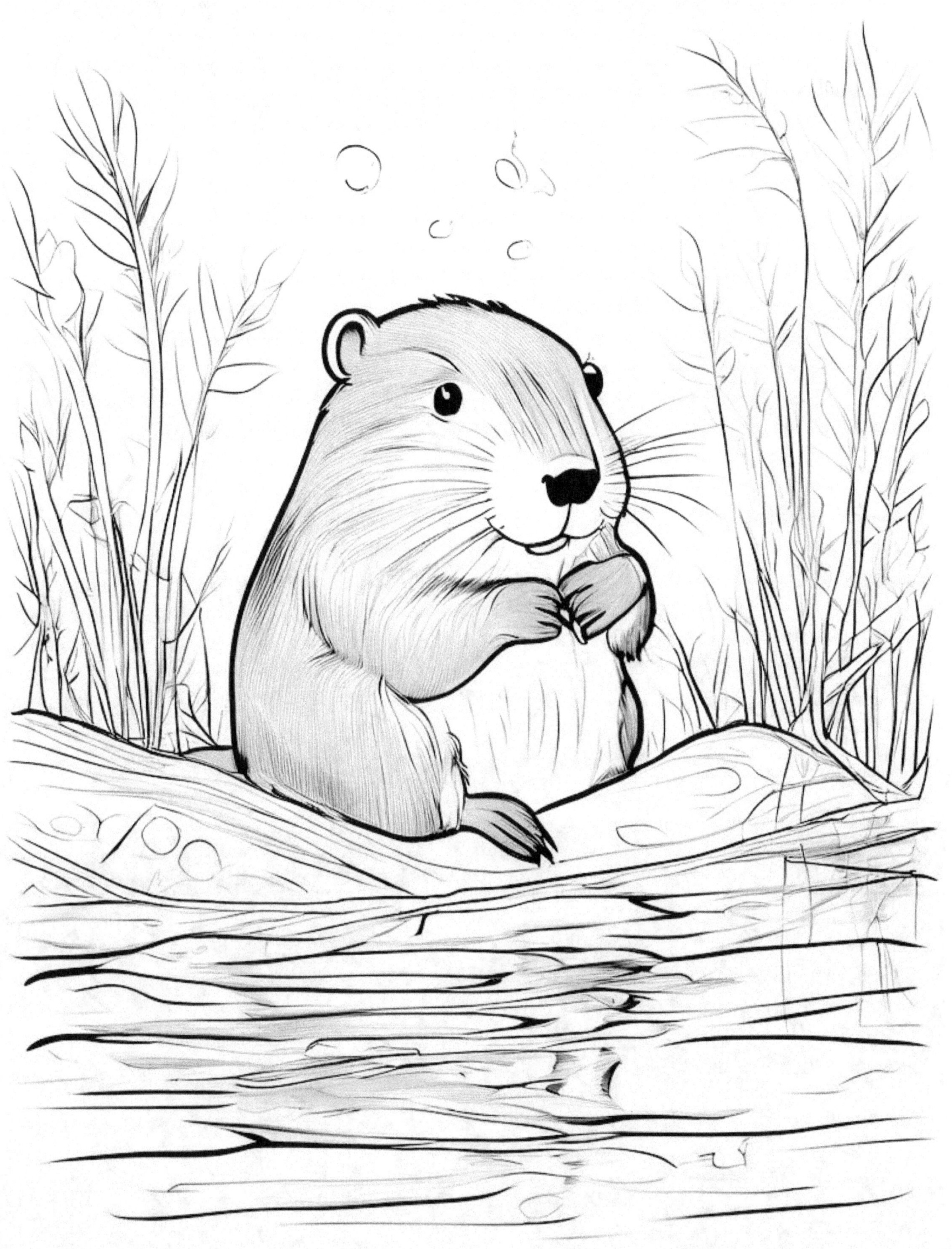

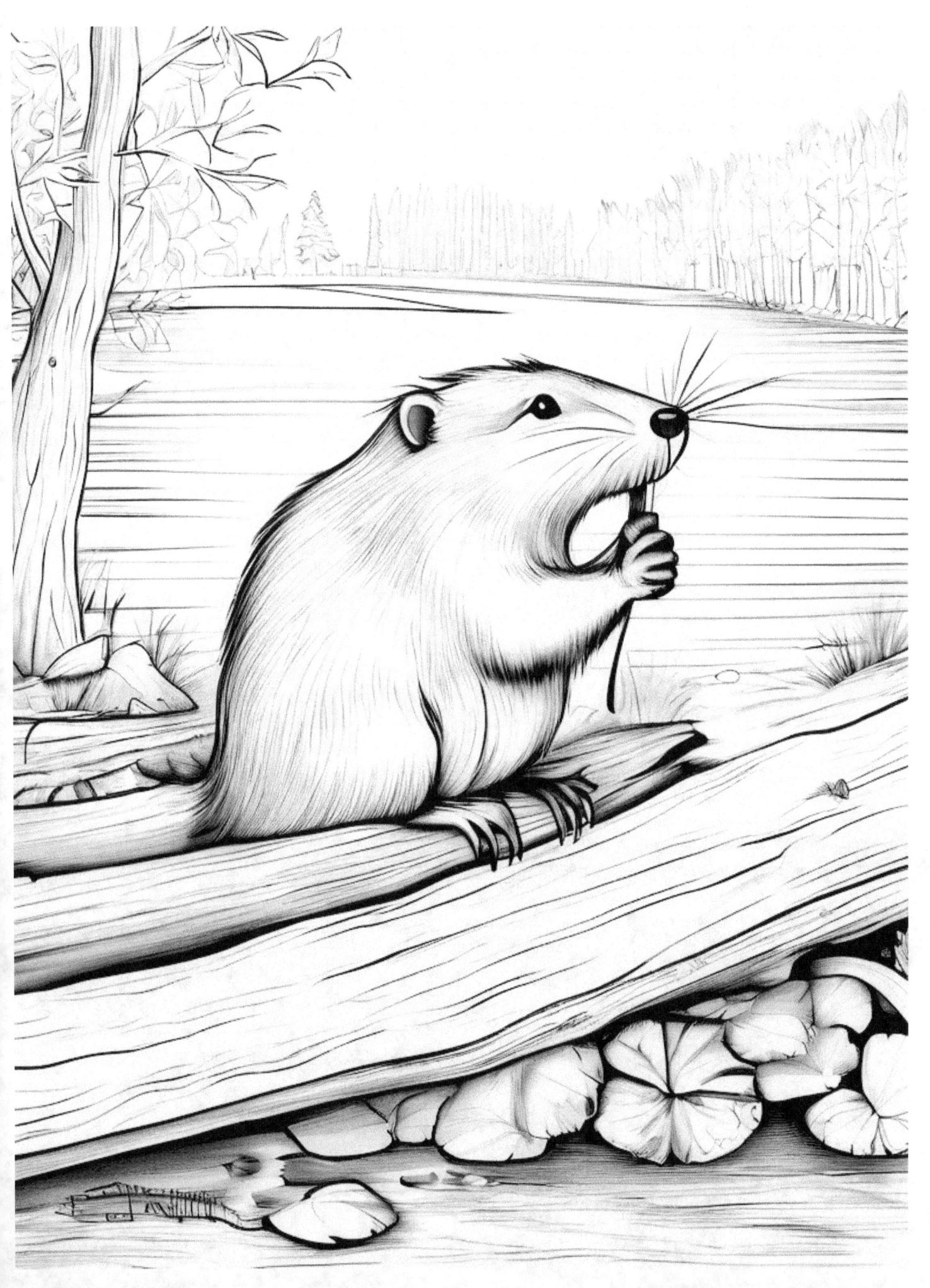

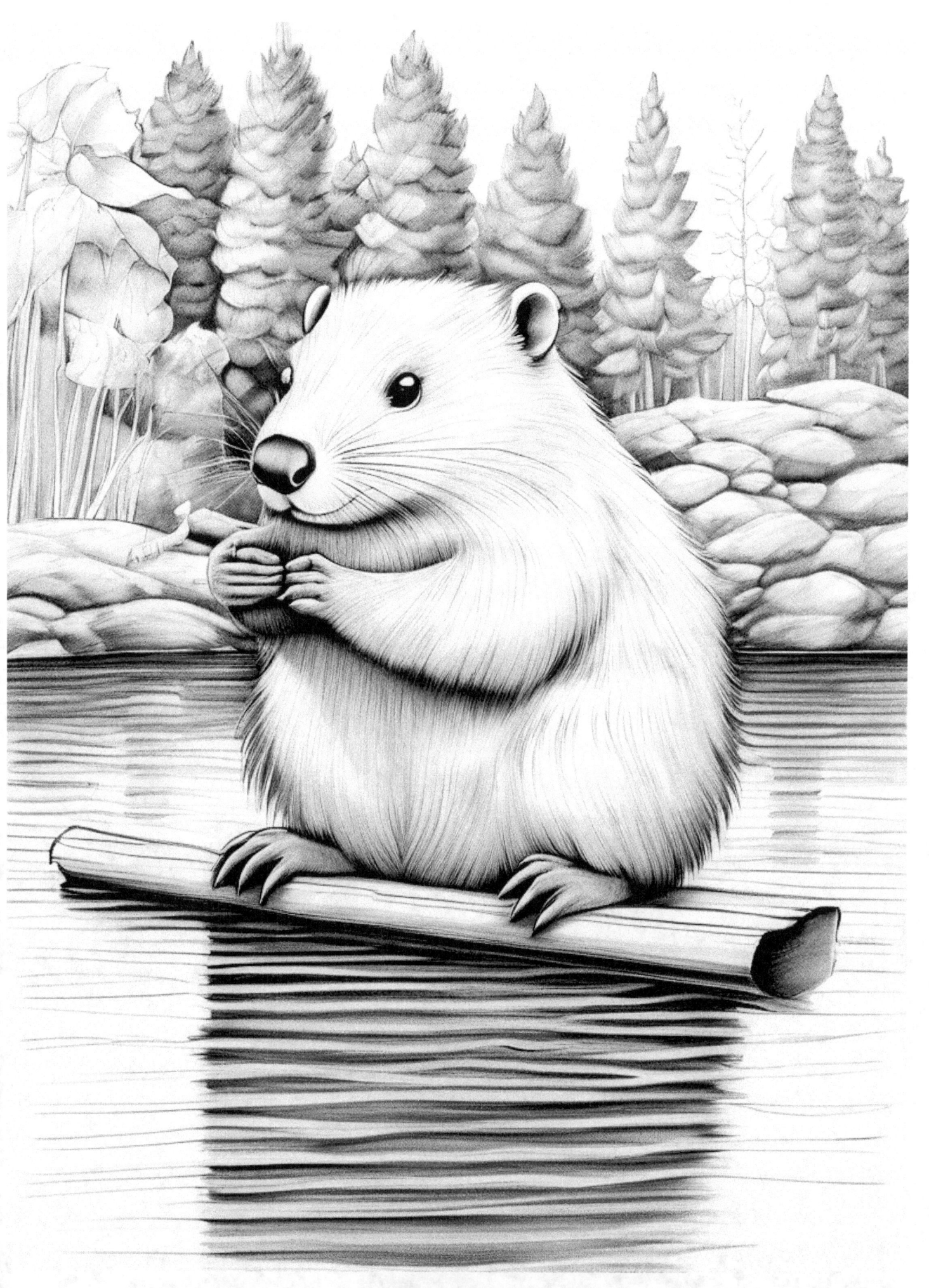

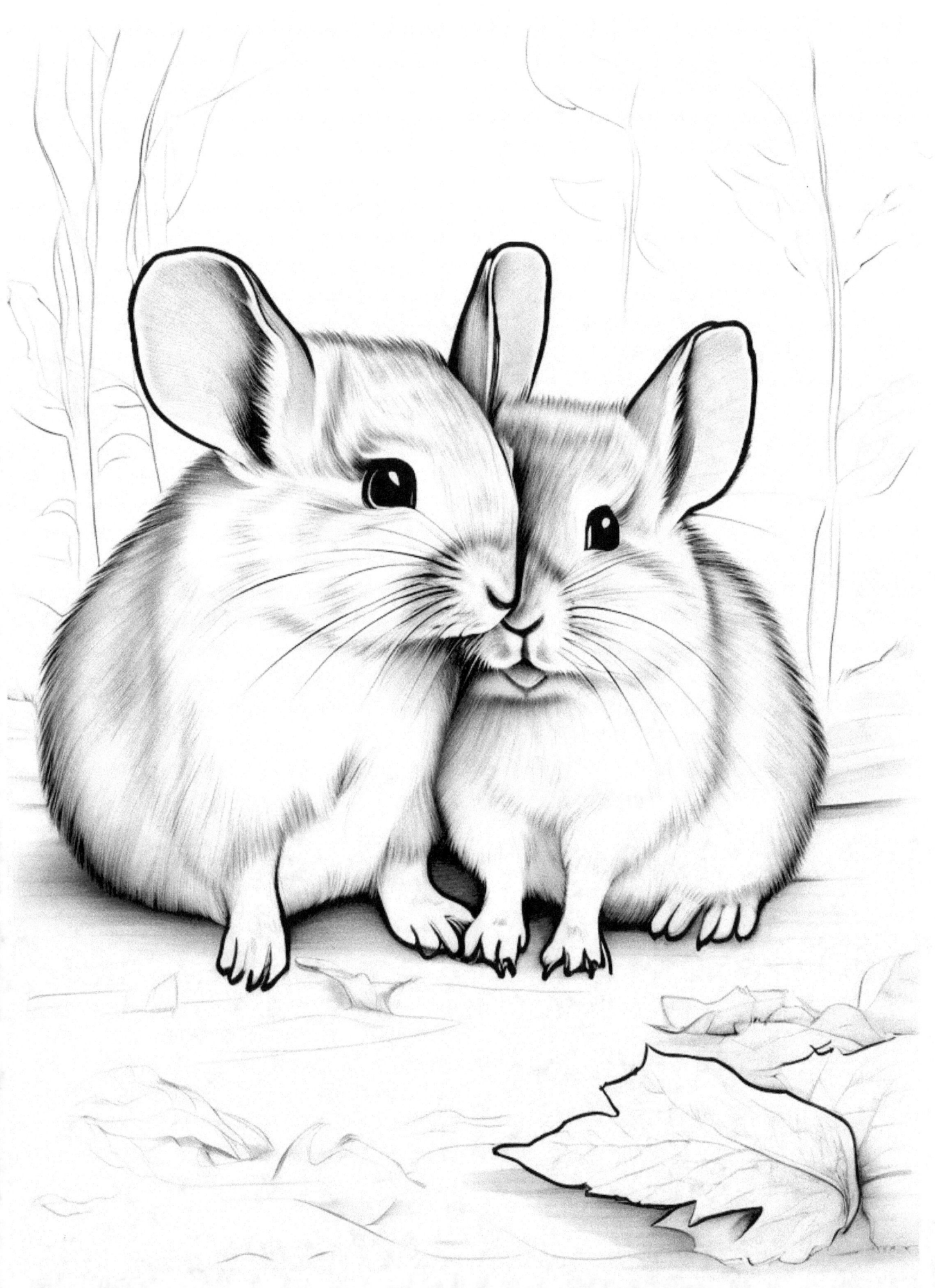

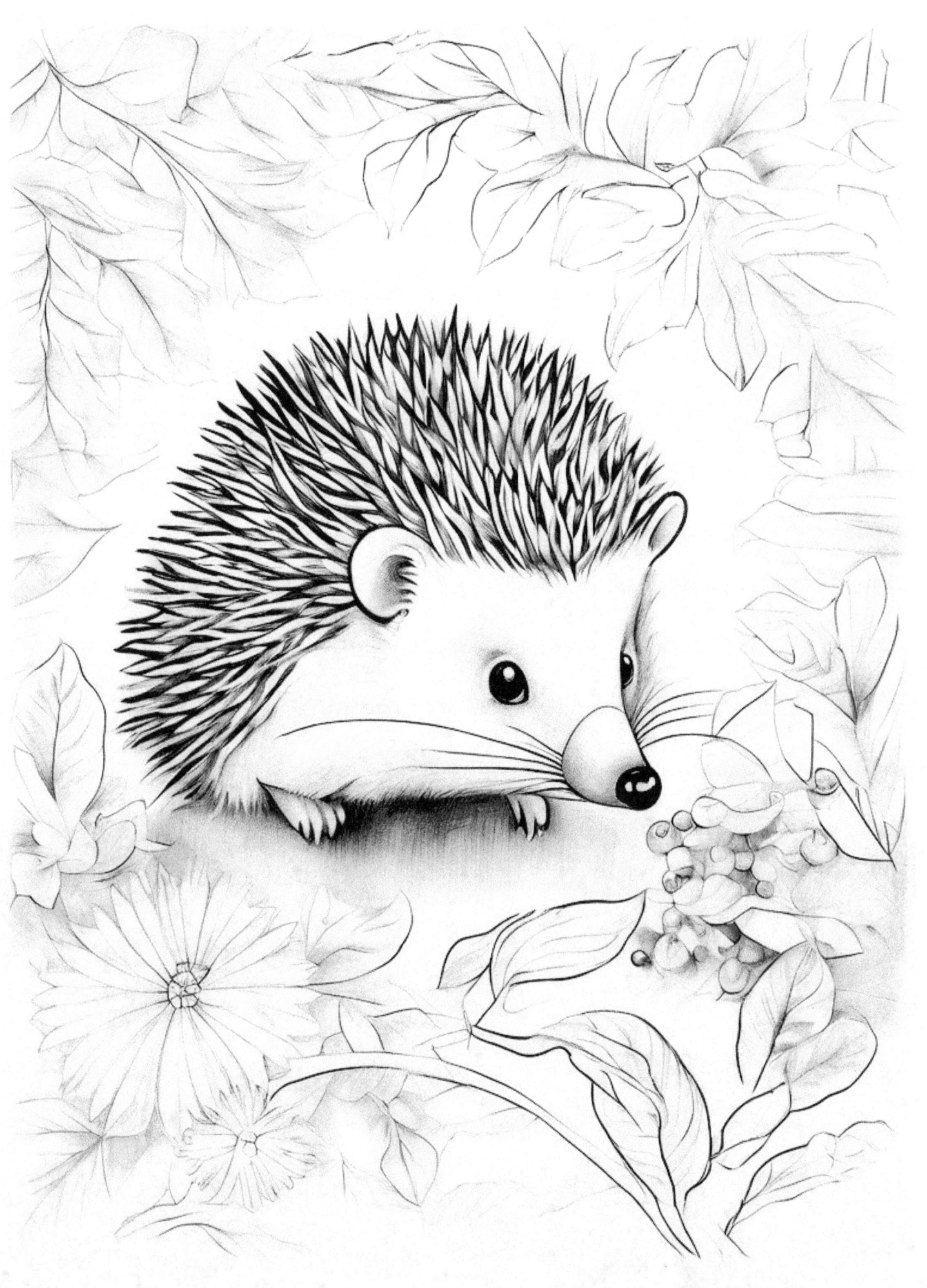

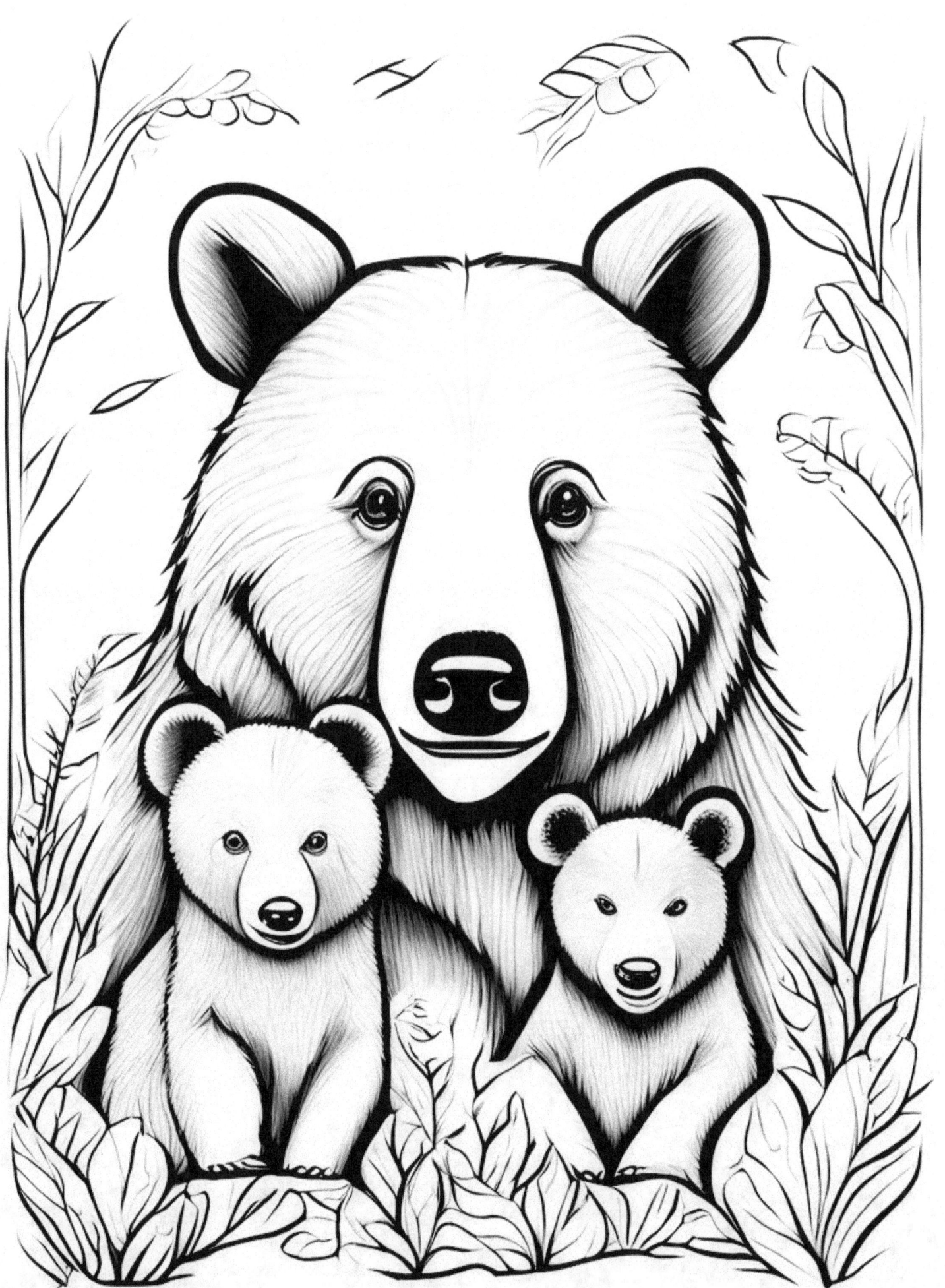

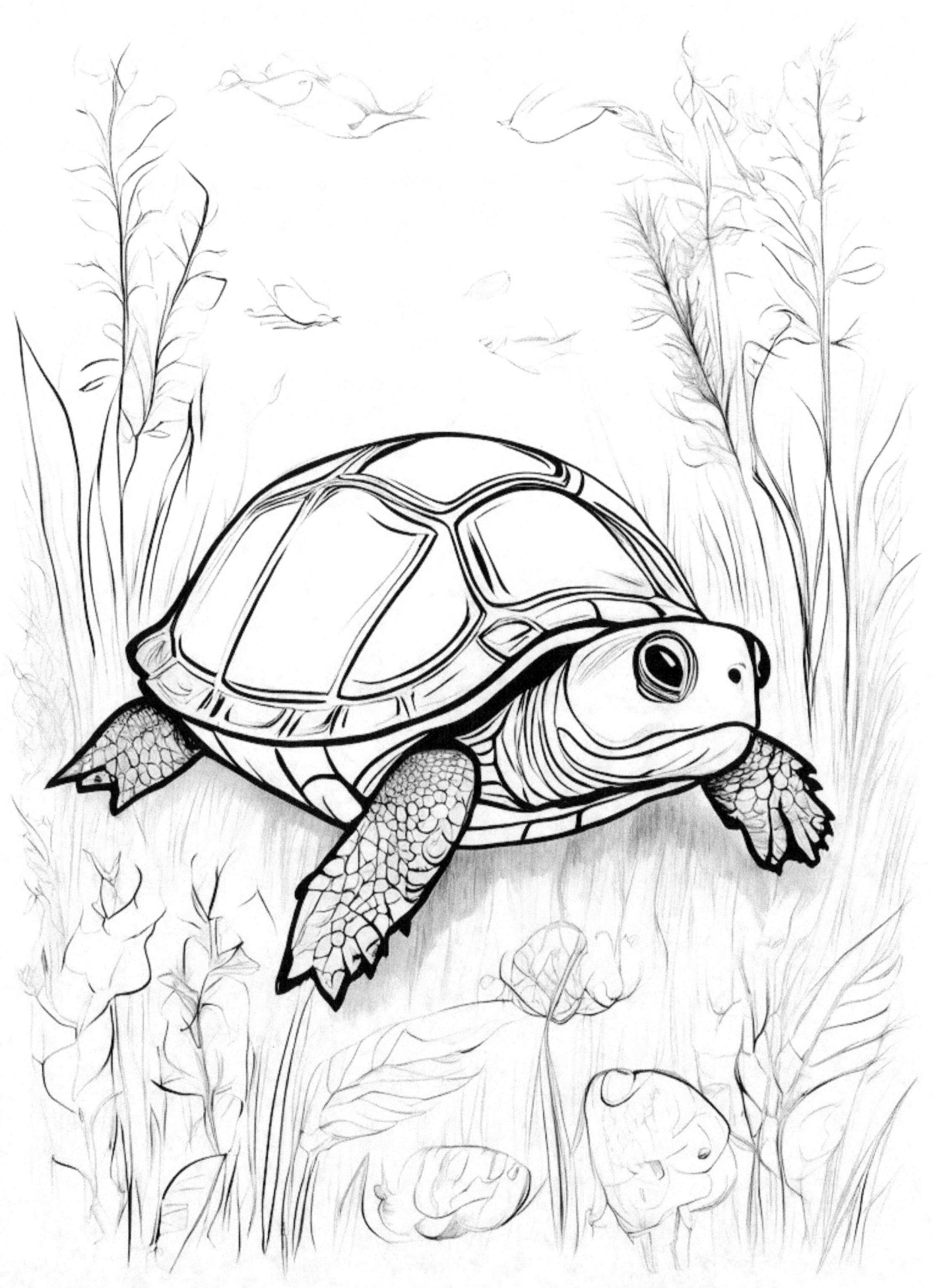

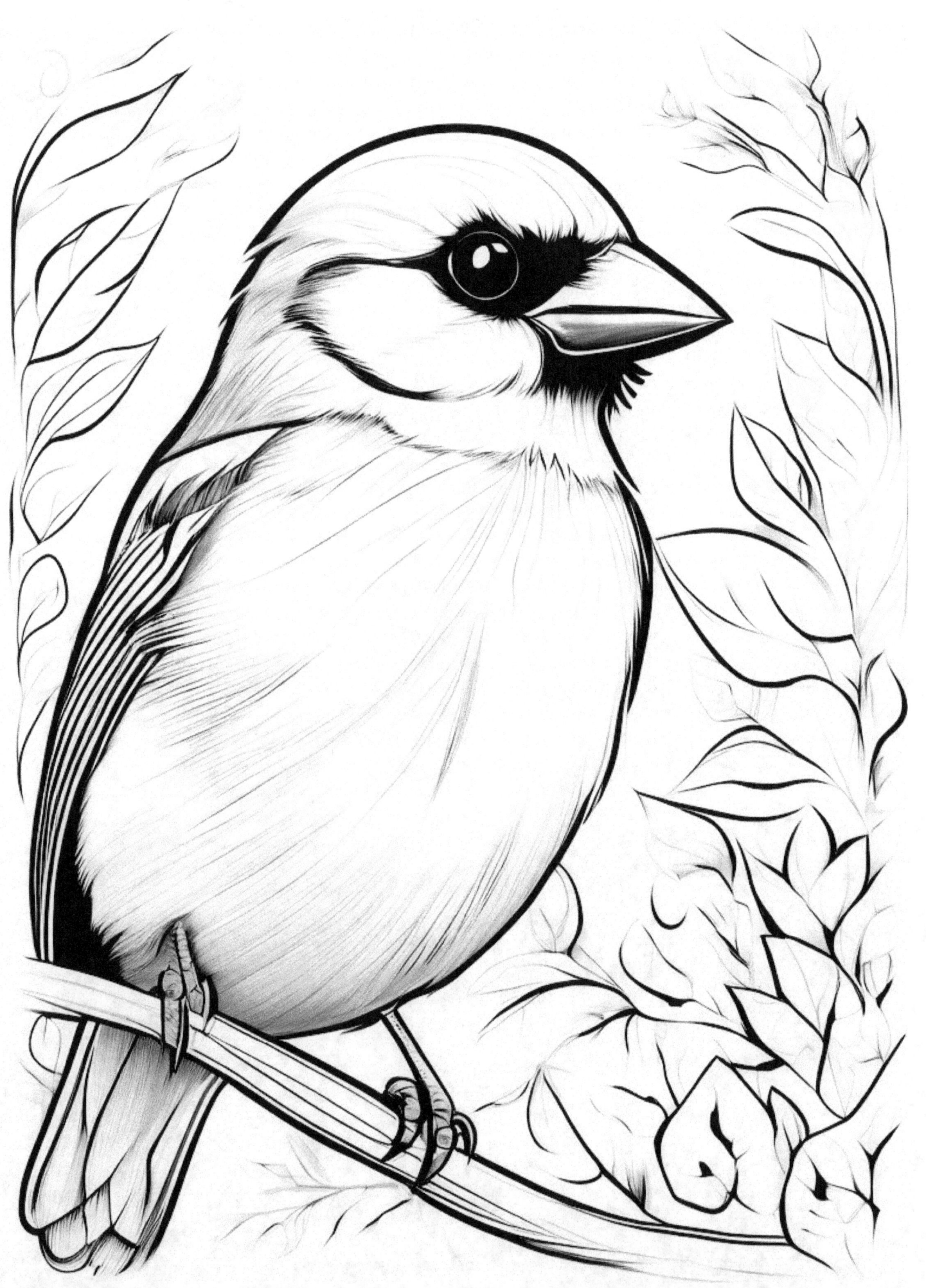

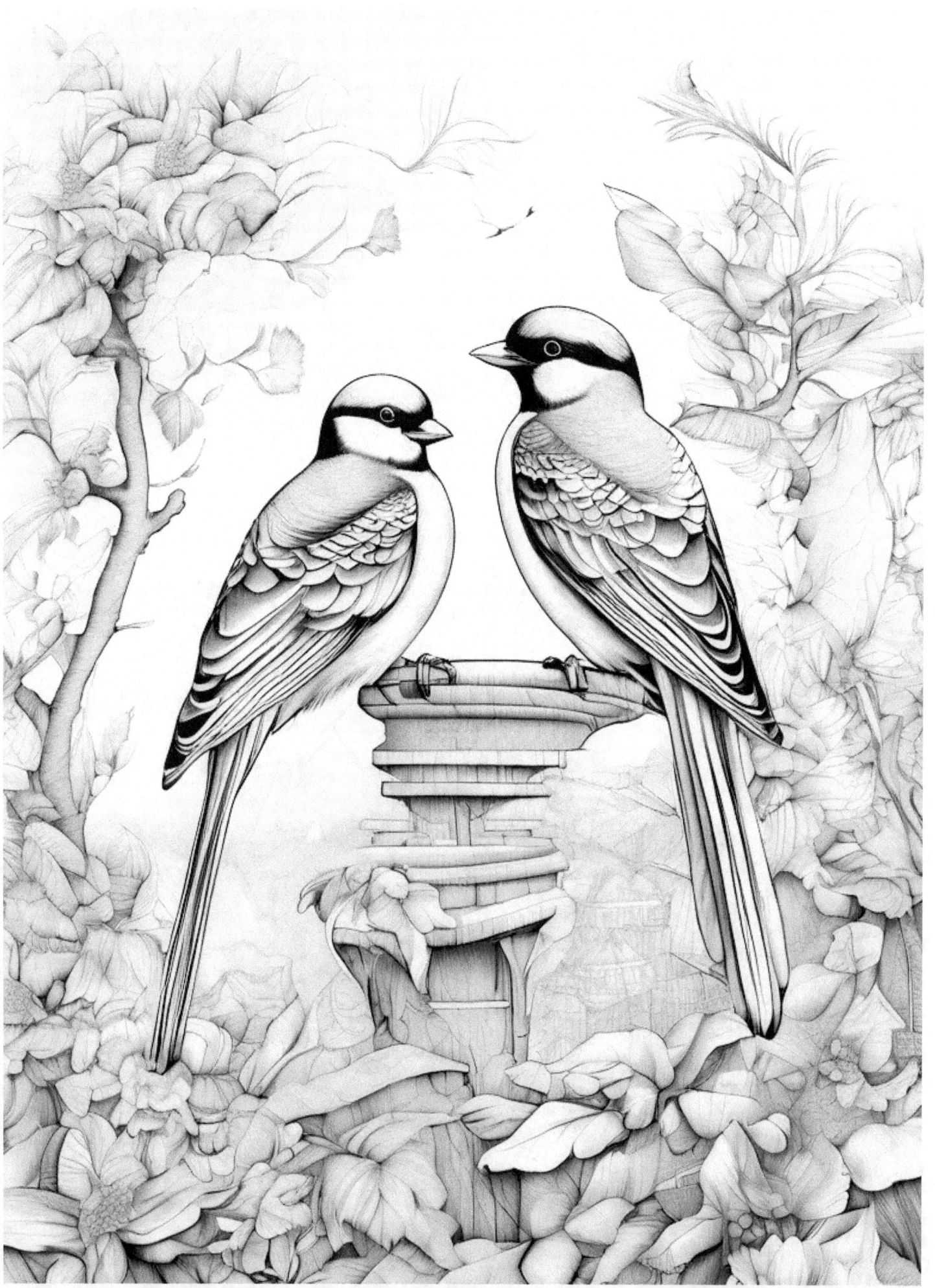

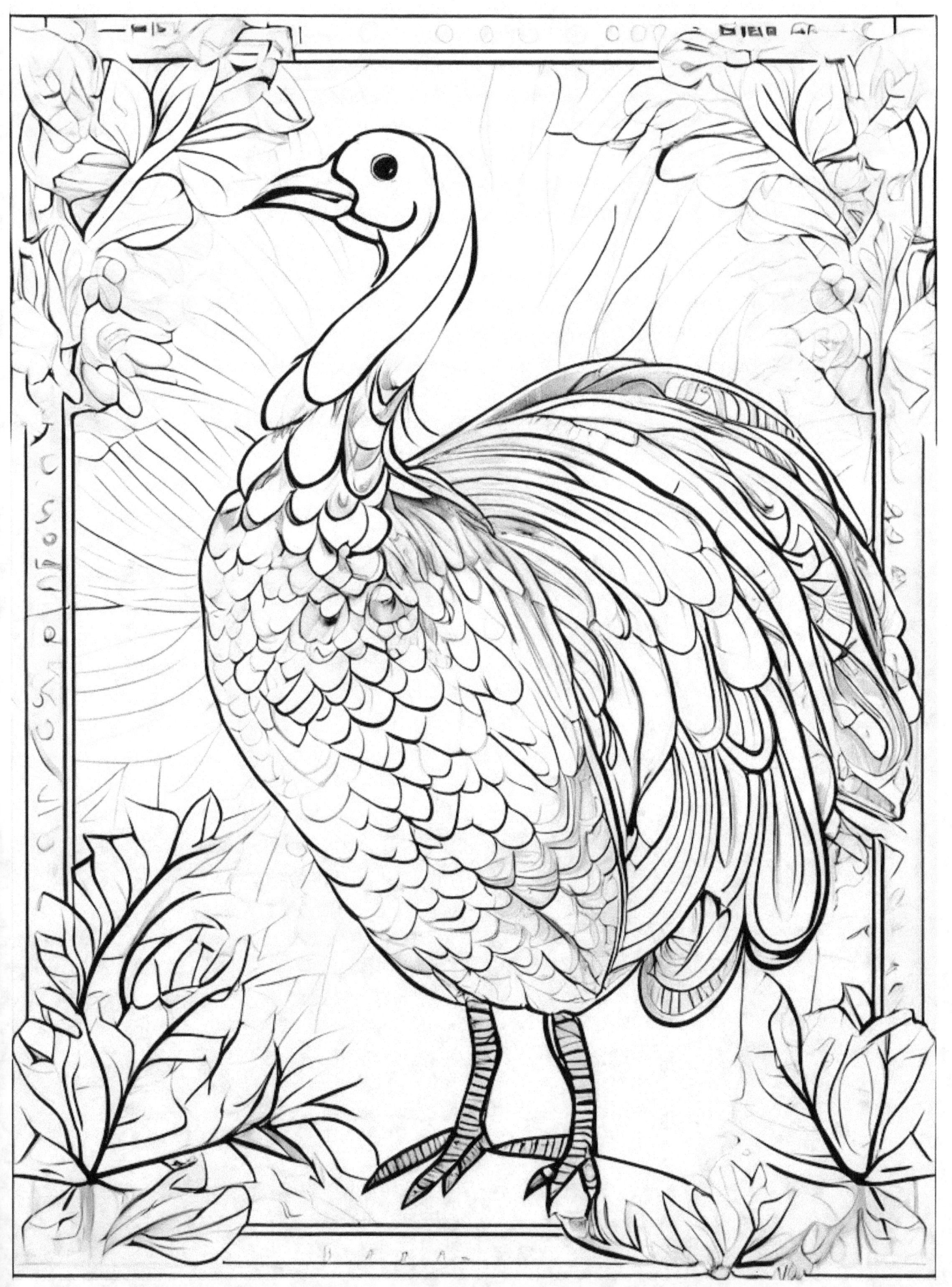

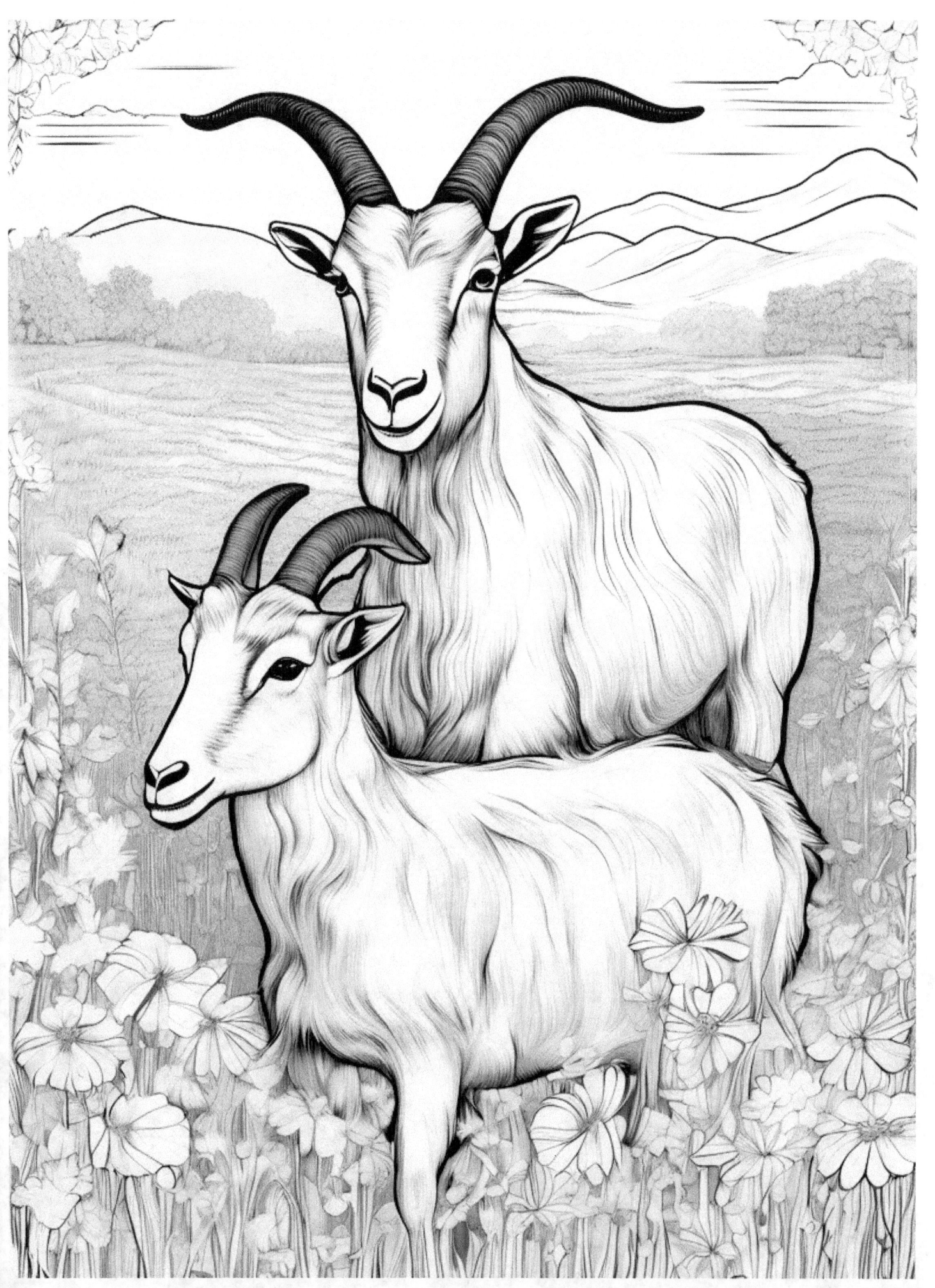

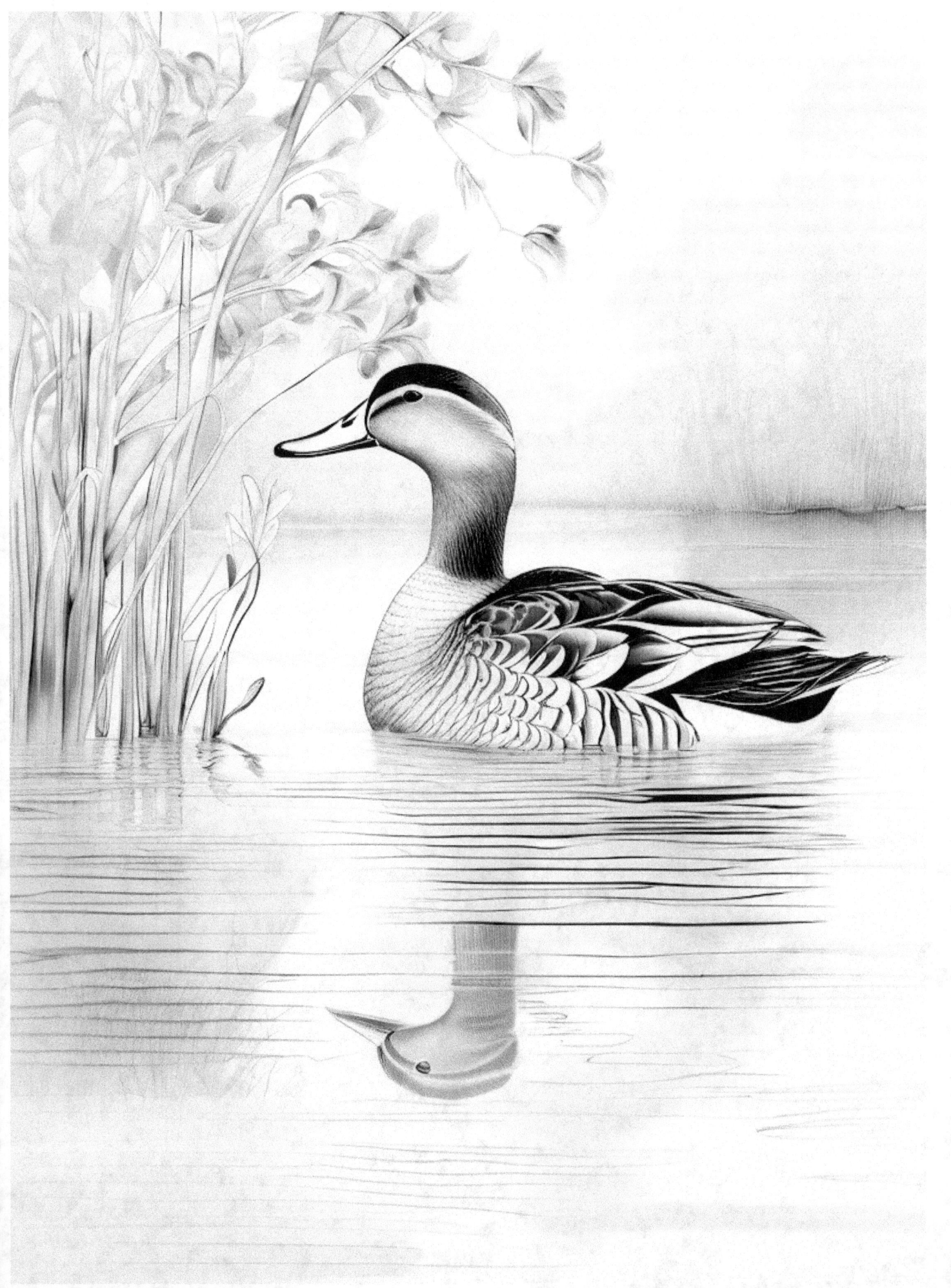

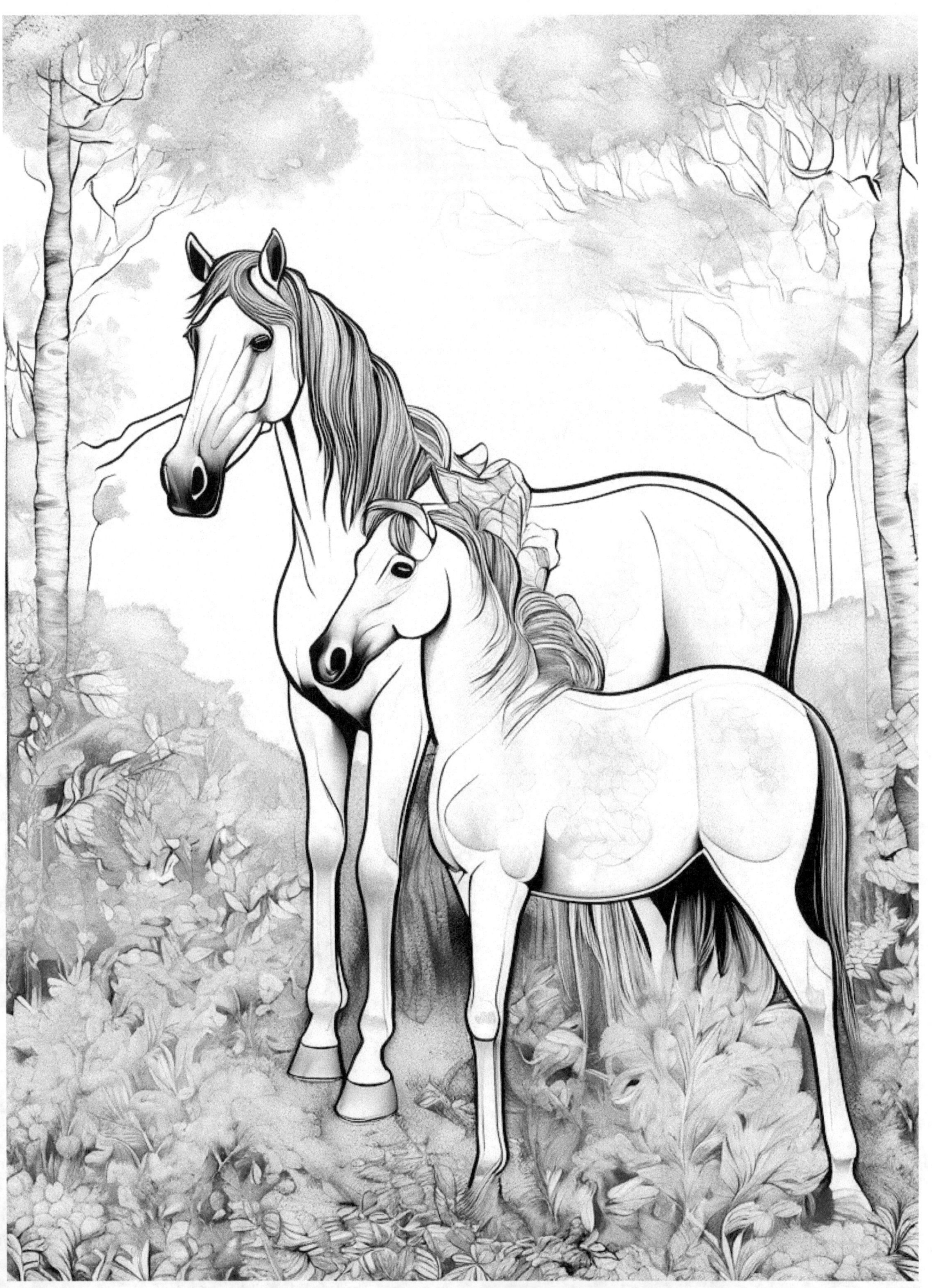

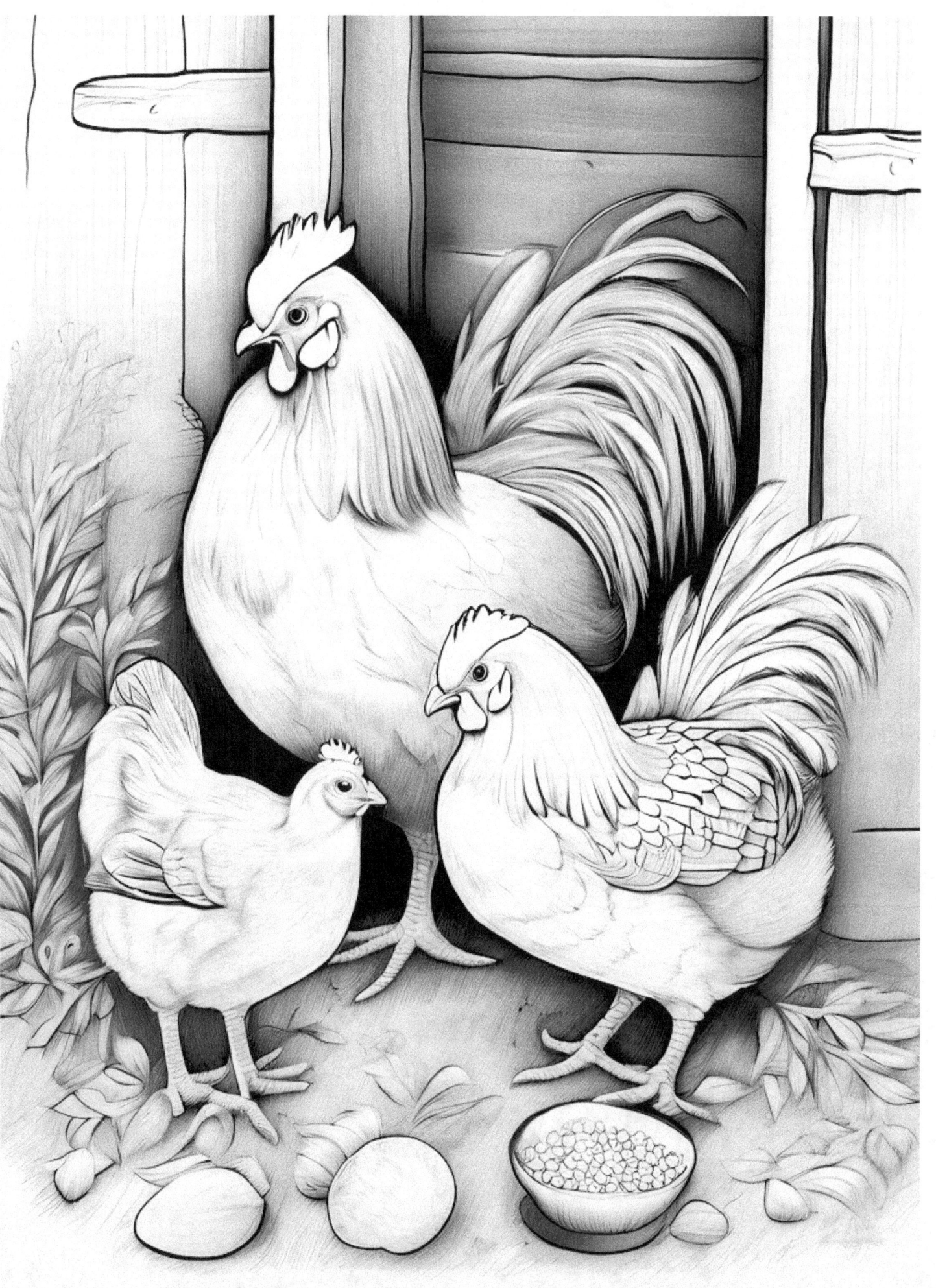

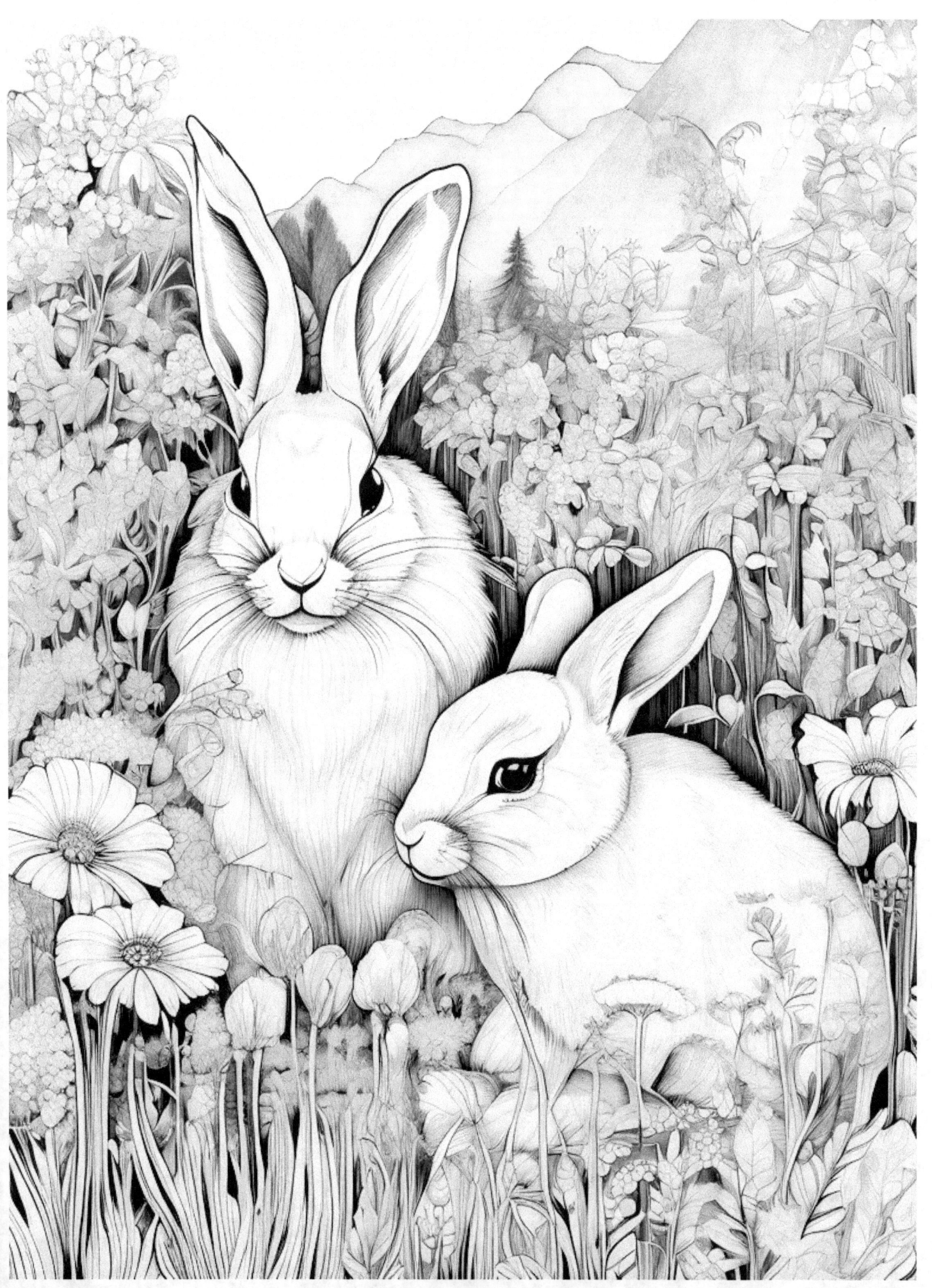

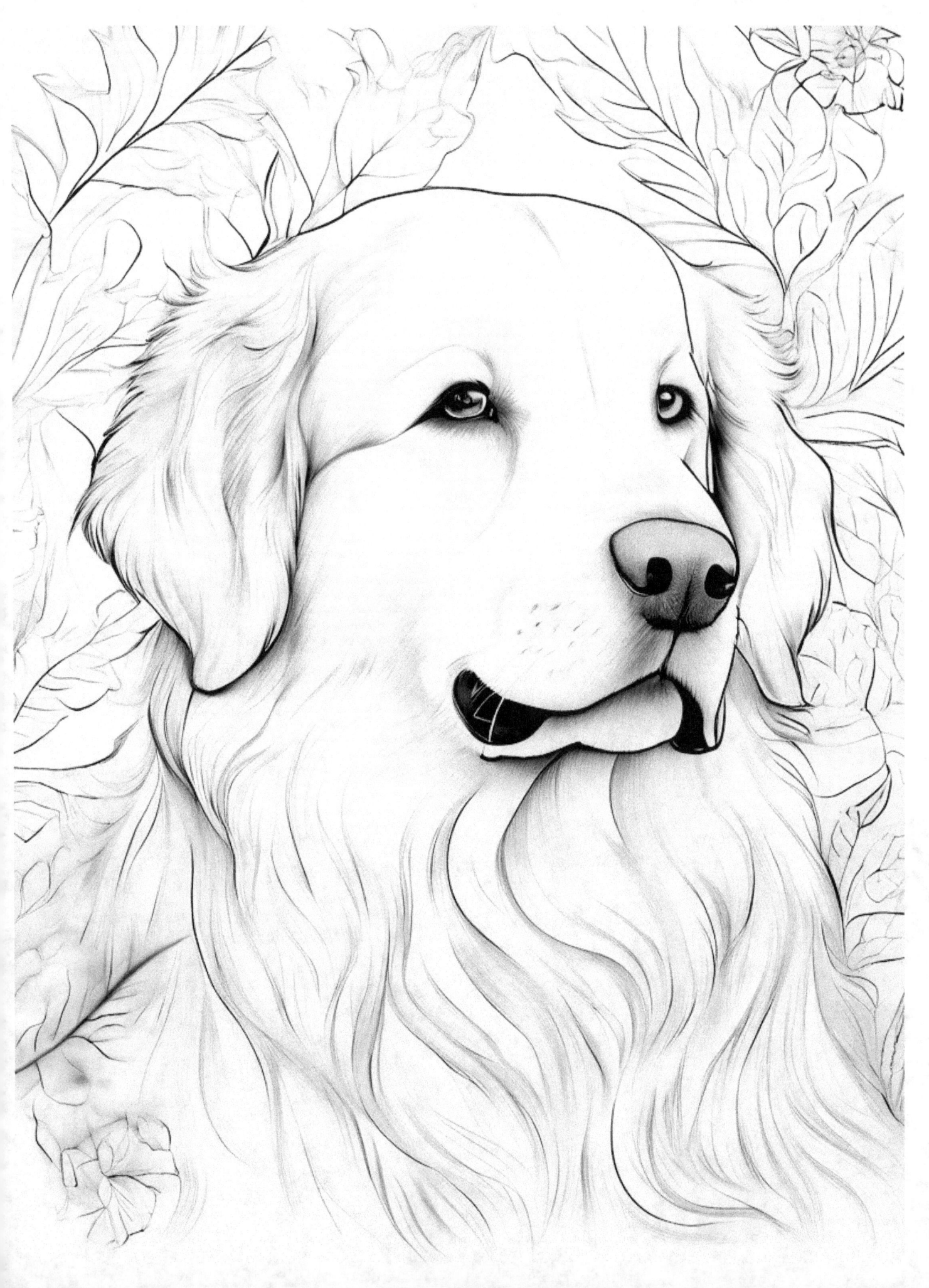

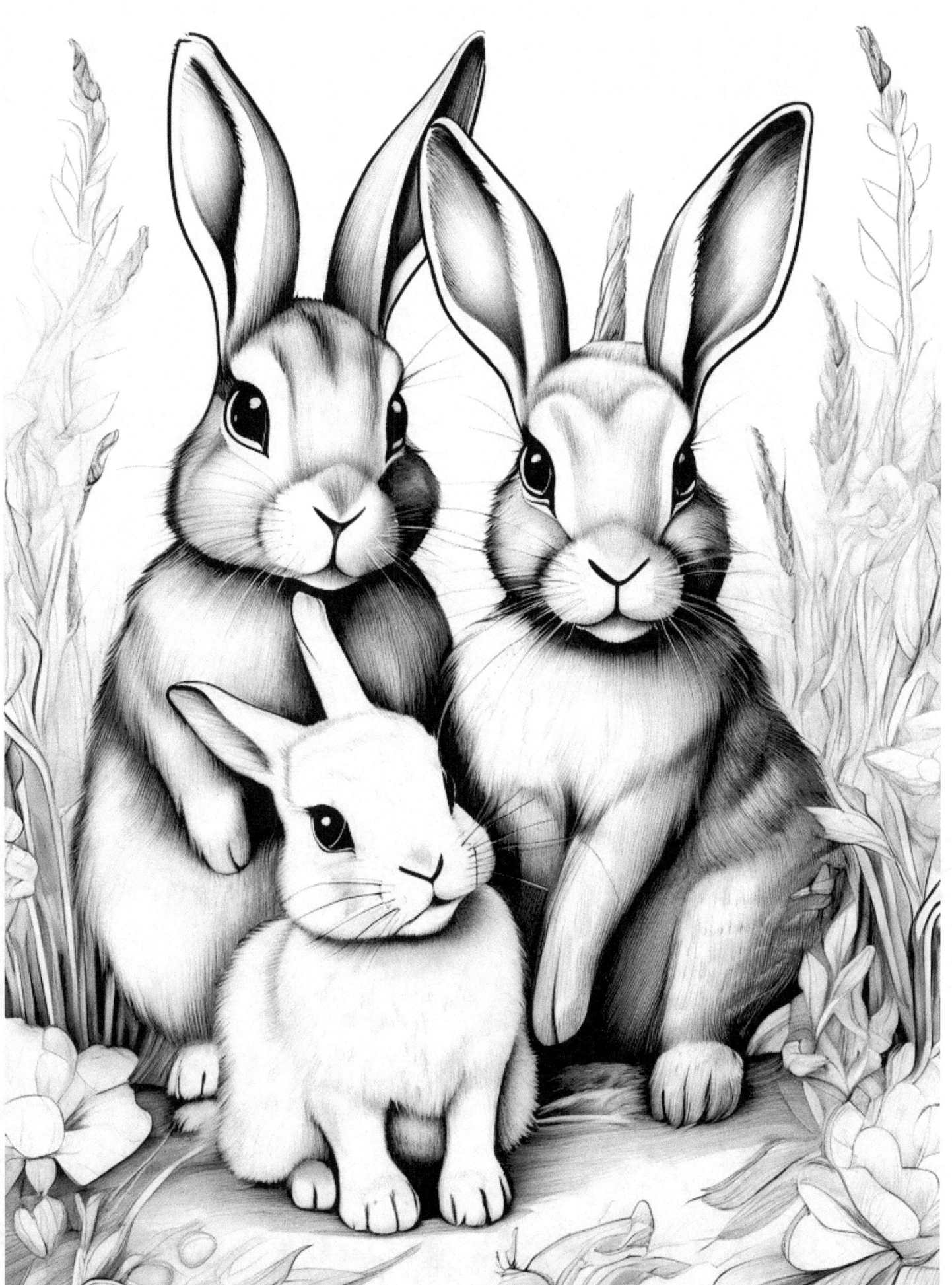

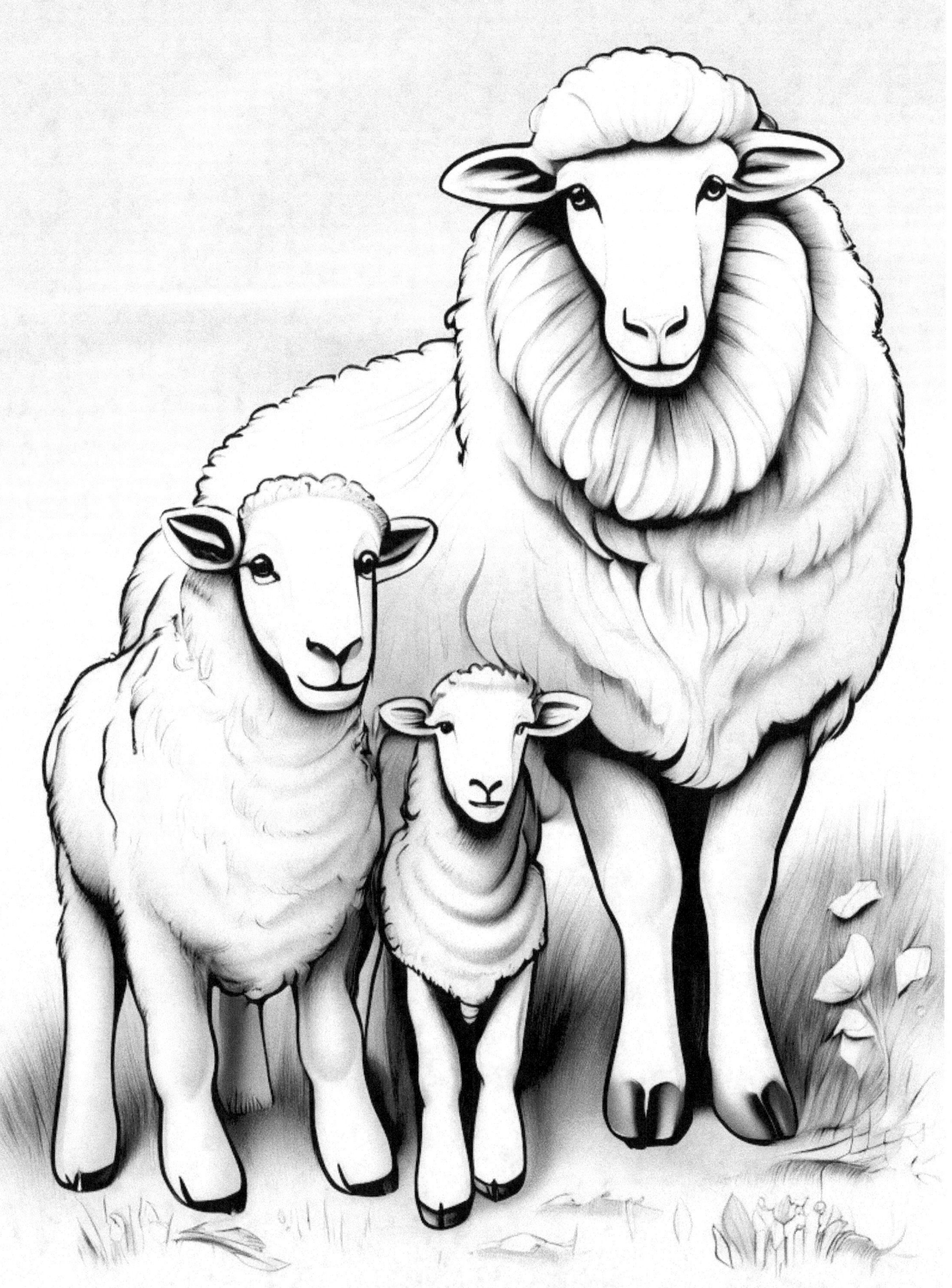

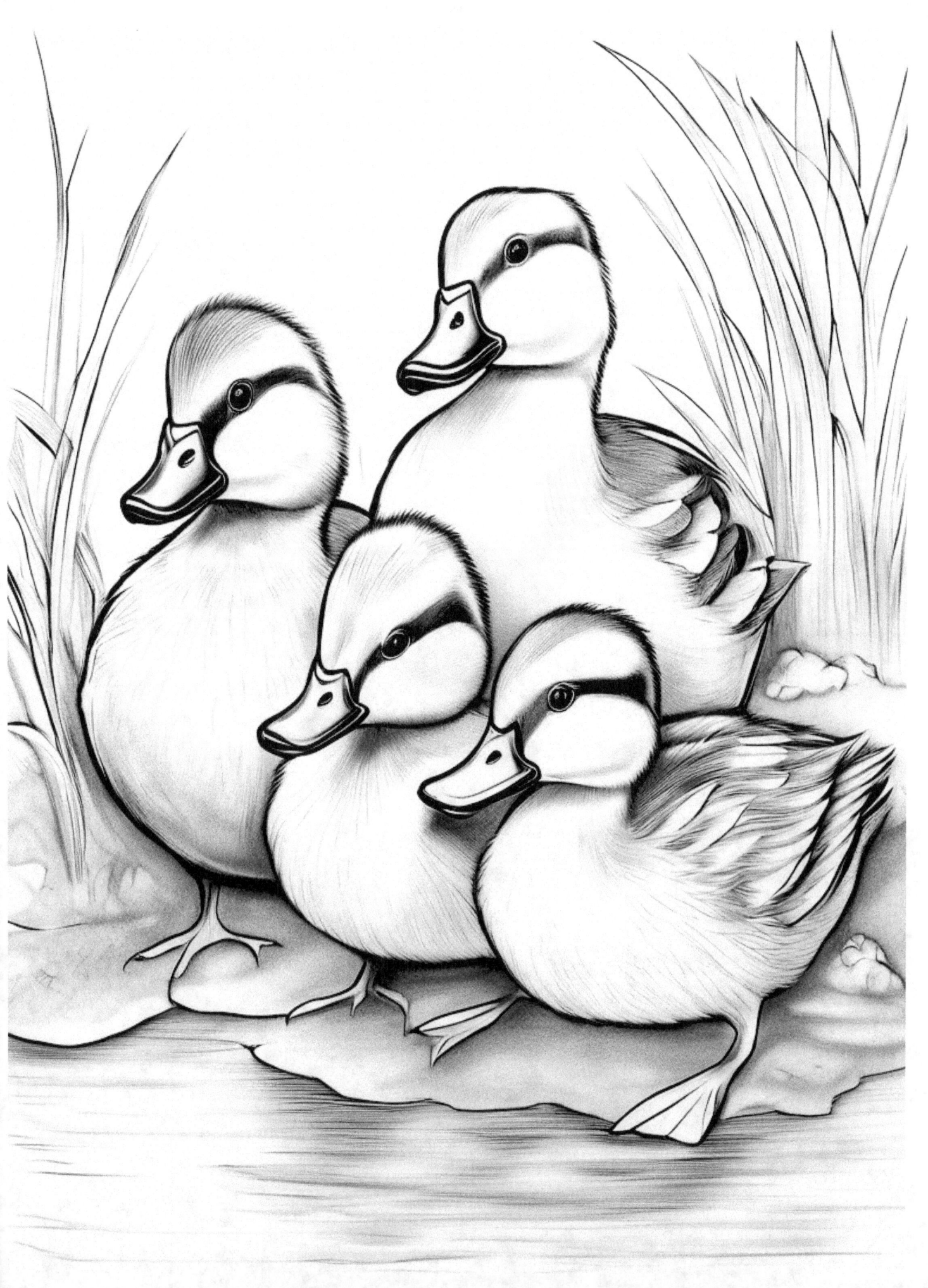

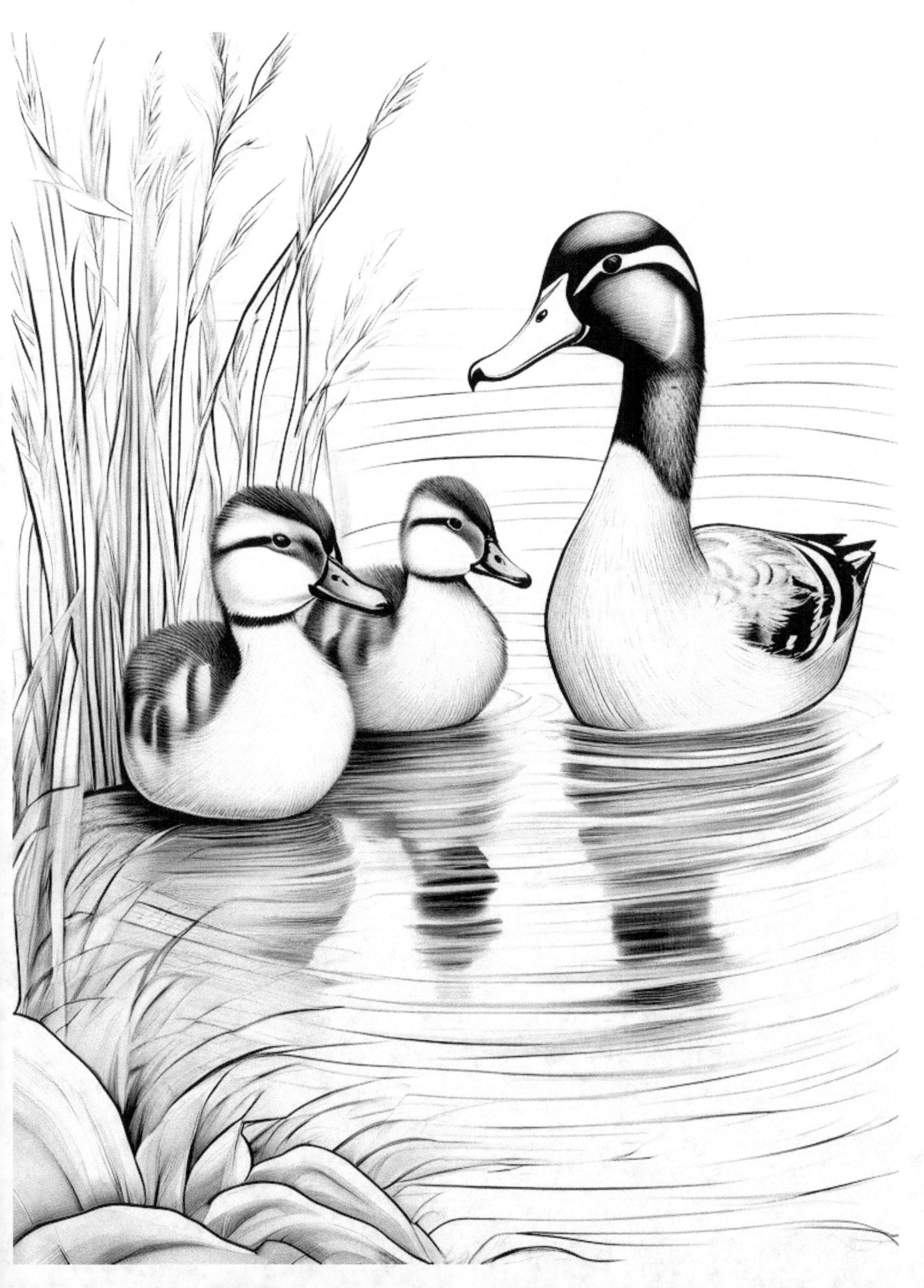

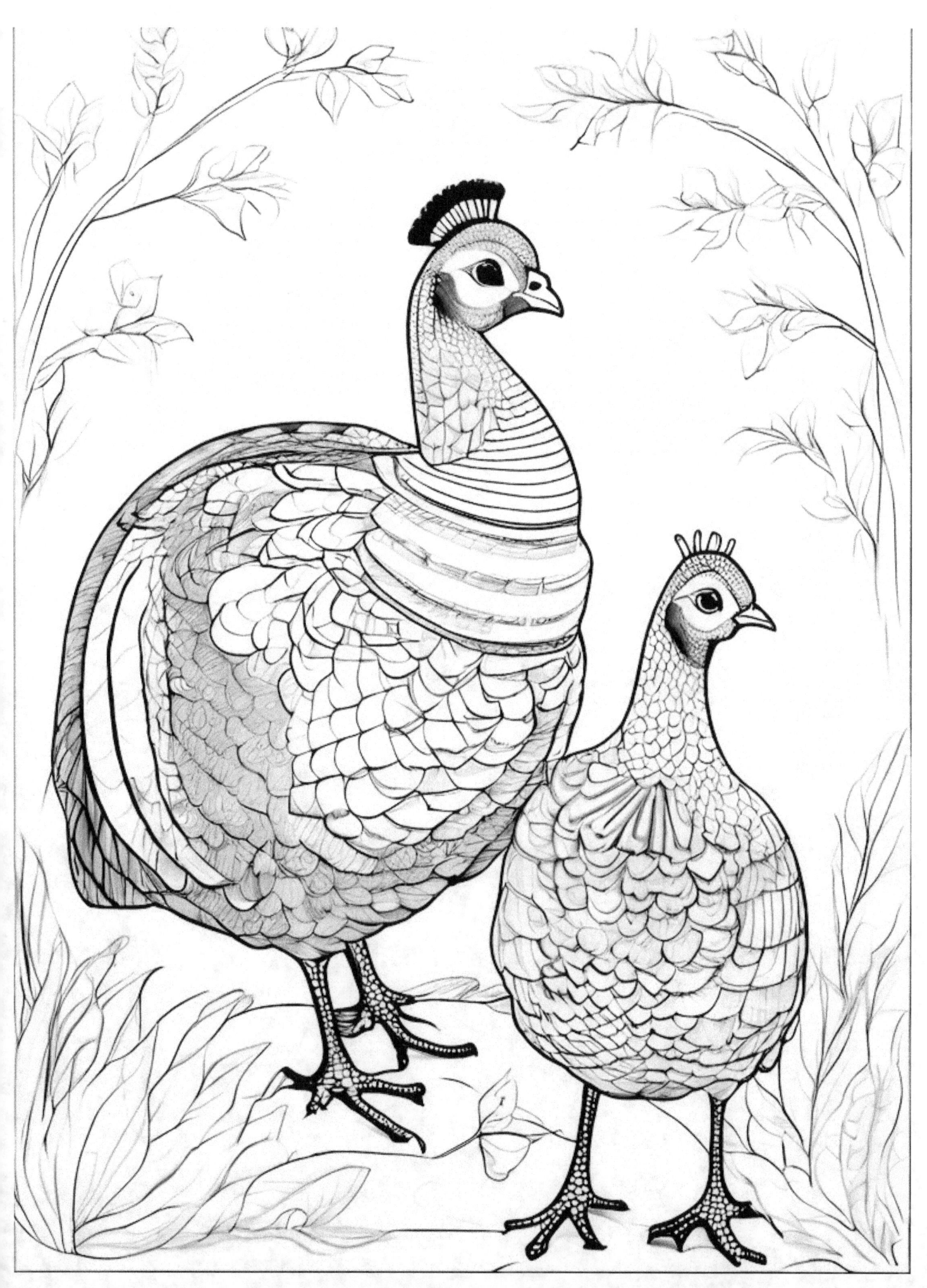

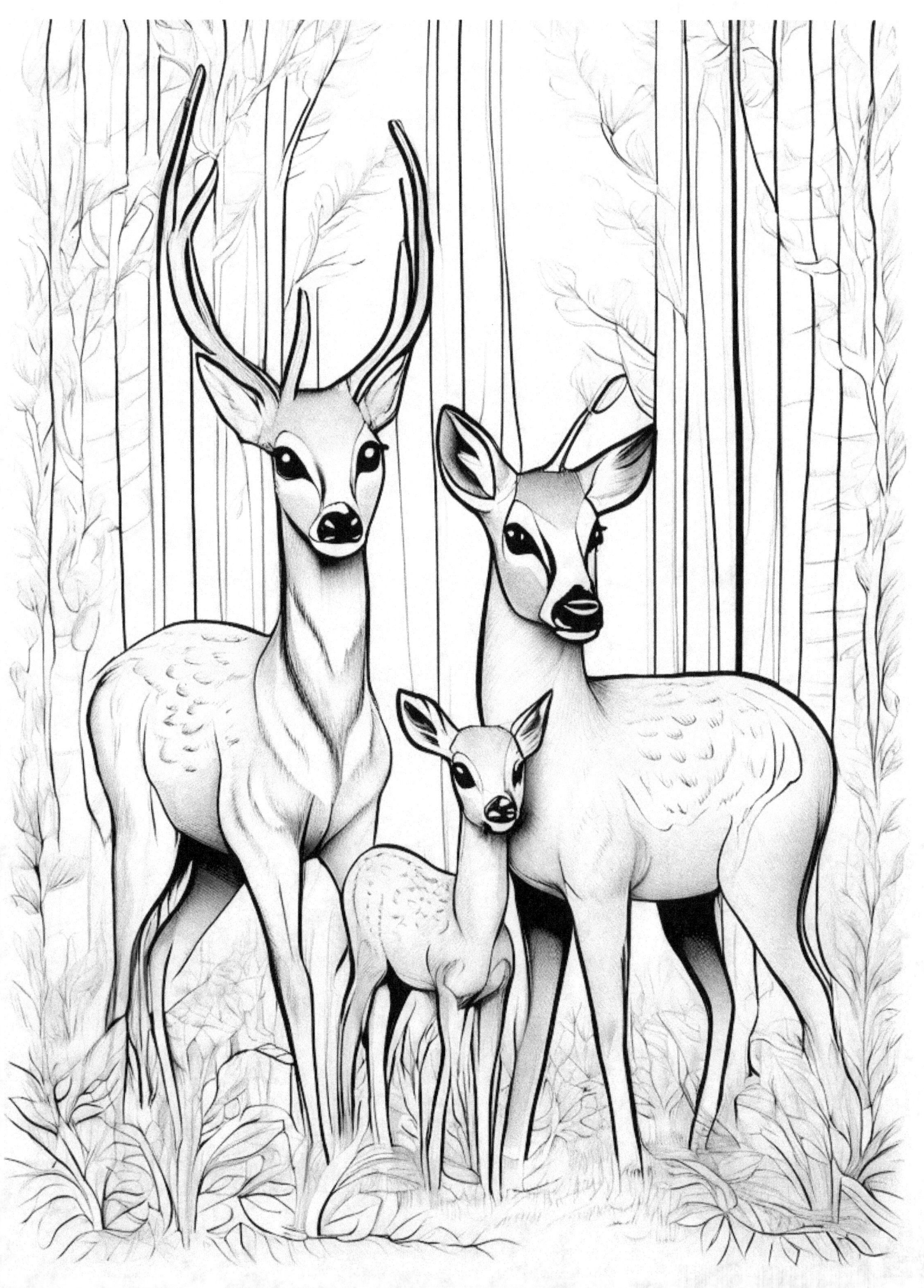

www.ingramcontent.com/pod-product-compliance
Lightning Source LLC
Chambersburg PA
CBHW082344220526
45470CB00008B/2639